Return from the Abyss
by Ian Paul Lomax
ISBN: 978-0-9929955-8-4

2

Return from the Abyss
by Ian Paul Lomax
ISBN: 978-0-9929955-8-4

All Rights Reserved.
No reproduction, copy or transmission of the publication may be made without written permission. No paragraph or section of this publication may be reproduced copied or transmitted save with the written permission or in accordance with the provisions of the Copyright Act 1956 (as amended)
Copyright 2015 Ian Paul Lomax.
The right of Ian Paul Lomax to be identified as the author of this work has been asserted in accordance with the Copyright Designs and Patents Act 1988
A copy of this book is deposited with the British Library

Published by

i2i Publishing. Manchester.
www.i2ipublishing.co.uk

By the same author: For the love of Christopher i2i May 2014

Prologue

On a cold winter's night in January 1958 in Withington Hospital, Manchester, my mother was delivered of a second son. The old maternity hospital had originally been a Victorian workhouse and it did not take much imagination to visualise the ragged inmates of an earlier time shivering their nights away in the stark conditions of the time.

I was christened Ian Paul Lomax, and little did my parents know the extreme peaks and troughs of life to which I would be subject. However, that is why I decided to write this book.

Dedication

My mother my rock

I could not write this book without a special chapter about my mother. From the very first moment I opened my eyes and was held by her I felt her warmth and kindness.

I will never forget from the earliest age, when I was just four years old and I first felt the hand and anger of my father. Even then I observed the look of horror and sadness in my mother's eyes.

She held me in her arms and I sobbed. I felt so safe and comforted whenever she held me. She had suffered personal tragedy and pain in her earlier life and felt the hand of my father for as long as I could remember. She always put her children first no matter how much anguish she was suffering personally.

She rose early every morning, cleaning and cooking and ironing and always made sure that there was food on the table. She did part-time work as well as looking after my grandma who we called Little Nanny. The poor old lady had no legs and my mum used to nurse her as well as looking after us. I remember seeing my mum being sick in the toilet many times but she still went out to work and looked after the family. I remember seeing her slumped on the chair too many times, in a state of exhaustion.

I used to look at her with a smile on my face and I always kissed her on the cheek.

She always protected me from my father even though she often suffered the consequences. She tried her best to keep me on the straight and narrow and fought my corner in the courts for my rebellious ways. Many times I saw her crying and not just because of my father, but also because of me and the troubles I used to get into. That is something I will always regret. Throughout my life she has always been there for me; always fed me when I had been short and given me money whenever I needed it.

I remember when I ran away to Paris at fourteen years old how she suffered and cried every day I was away. She thought the worst especially when the police were searching for me and it would be nearly four days before she knew I was safe.

Later on after I had eventually left home, I would always go back and see her, whenever I could. She was my hero, a fighter, protector and a loving mum.

I will truly love her forever for always being there for me and for fighting my corner in the Greek courts. I am truly grateful for everything she has done for me.

She is a mum in a million and I'm so proud of her and I will love her till my dying day.

Mum thank you for giving me life and protecting me and standing my corner; you're the bravest of the brave.

I will love you always.

Your loving son Ian xxxxx

Mother

From the very first moment I opened my eyes
She held me close.
Her warm embrace kept me safe.
Her loving smiles
Her loving ways
Her love never faltered
A heart full of gold

She suffered pain and sadness
She showed such strength
Through her loving ways
My mother I thank you
My mother I love you
Always my strength
My mum

Acknowledgements

I would also like to thank my step father **Jack** (R.I.P.) for giving me love and affection and standing by me in the Greek courts.

My dear wife **Suzi** for her love & support.

My English children **Amy-Louise** and **Adam** for the love and pleasure they give me.

My Greek son **Christopher** who I miss so much; separated by land and sea..

My sisters **Diane, Pat** and **Denise**.

My brothers **Mark, Stephen** and **Derek** .

My friends **Adrian Jones, Susan Jones, Andy Hart, Andy Hill, Pete Stott, Mark Slater, Graham Grant** for their encouragement to write this book.

My football mates **Joe Cooke, Steven Cooke** and **Fred Dickinson** a true legend and a gentleman .

My publisher **Lionel Ross of i2i Publishing** for keeping me in focus and for all his generous advice.

My final thoughts go to the memory of **my father** whose abuse and actions against me may have made me rebellious and sent me down the wrong paths. However, he, by his actions made me the stronger and more determined person I am today.

8

Chapter One

The hand that rocked the cradle

My father was only small and slim with short black hair. He was handsome but he had dark secrets. He loved his drink and gambling and he was a bad loser. I used to dread him coming home after he had had a drink and had been gambling as he used to take his losses out on me and my mother.

I suffered many a time with his anger and wrath and had the scars and bruises to prove it.

I remember my father being in and out of my life when I was a young child. My mother used to tell me that my dad was working away. I didn't find out until I was much older that his absences were because he was in and out of prison.

When he was in my life I suffered with his cruelty and his constant bullying. This carried on right through my school days. I couldn't count the number of times I went to school with bruises and cried with my head on my school desk.

Why he bullied me so much I will never understand. I wasn't allowed to play with friends like a normal child. I was always locked up in my room. I lost count of the number of times I sneaked out of my box-room window to meet up with my pals.

When I was allowed out, I was constantly getting into trouble with the local Bobbies. At the top of my road in Highfield, which was an estate in Farnworth, there used to be a row of police houses. One local Bobbie there was infamous. His name was Sergeant Swann and he later became a thorn in my side.

Anyway, back to the story.

When I was four years old I remember sitting on the table in the kitchen. I was just playing with my mother as young children do, when my father walked in. For whatever reason, I still do not know until this day, he punched me on the nose. The force was so great that my head hit the back of the wall and blood was pouring out of my nose.

I will never forget the look on my father's face; it was pure hatred. I remember crying and my mother's look of fear still haunts me to this very day.

This was the first punch and many more followed over the years. It only stopped when I was sixteen and I had had enough of his constant beatings. I faced up to him and gave him a good hiding. He never touched me or my mother again after that.

I came into the world in Withington hospital which was in Didsbury, Manchester.

When I was nearly two years old we moved to Lee Street in an old mill town called Farnworth; part of the borough of Bolton.

Lee Street was your typical cobbled street with pre-war houses with outside toilets in the back yards. I very rarely visited the toilet after six o'clock in the evening as I was too scared to go out. There was no lighting and I was afraid of the dark. So my younger brother's potty came in very useful at the time.

The house we lived in was a three up and two down. It was a typical terrace house of the time.

My bedroom was quite large. There were three small beds for me and my two brothers. They were Derek who was seven years older than me and Mark my younger brother.

The wallpaper was quite plain with a flowered pattern and we had cream curtains. The floor covering was just a plain brown carpet and was very thin. There wasn't much of a view out of the window as there was a large empty factory building facing us in the back street. I and my brothers used to play there most days.

In my sisters' room which was a bit smaller; there were two beds, one each for my sisters Diane and Pat.

The girls' room was much better decorated than ours. It had pink wallpaper with flowers on and a nice cream carpet with pink curtains hanging on the window.

It was sparsely furnished with a wardrobe and bedside cabinets which we all shared.

My mum and dad's bedroom was quite pleasant; she had cream flowered, patterned wallpaper with rich cream hanging curtains. There were a few pictures on the walls and a nice beige carpet.

There was a small kitchen in the house with a table and chairs a few cupboards. There was also a small pantry where my mother used to store the food.

The front room had a small couch and two chairs, a brown carpet with a small white rug; a glass cabinet in the corner and a small table with a black and white television.

My older sister Denise lived with my grandma as the house was too small for all of us and she only came to live with us when we moved to another house in Highfield in 1966.

Like a said, I very rarely saw my father in the early days which was a blessing for me so I could play out and have fun like normal children.

At that time in the early sixties in Lee Street you never saw much crime, so people felt safe and would leave their front doors open.

Most of the people in the street were elderly and were very friendly and everybody knew each other.

Every day you saw the elderly polishing their front steps and mopping up in front of their houses. They would shout to each other across the cobbled street asking if they would like a cup of tea, a biscuit and a chat.

Many times I remembered a certain lady called fat Hilda. She was elderly and must have been twenty five stone. She was forever knocking on the front door asking if she could borrow a few tea bags and a couple of spoons of sugar.

It was the norm in those days. We all lived in impoverished times but were happy nevertheless.

Every Wednesday the rag and bone man used to come round on his horse and cart and you could hear him in the street shouting, "rags and bones," at the top of his voice.

My mother then used to go out and look through the clothes he had on his cart and if she saw anything she liked and thought it fitted any of us, she would then barter with him and buy the item.

This used to be a regular thing every week with my mum. She still says to this day that we were always smartly dressed, which made me chuckle.

In those days if anybody in the street had children and they grew out of their clothes they would be passed on to nearby households who had younger children and put to good use.

It was around 1964 when I started to see more of my father. It was happy times for a while as he seemed to be a changed man. It was then that my younger brother Stephen was born.

The school I attended was in a wooden hut. It had only two classes and they were separated by a wooden wall.

In 1966, the year we won the World Cup, it was time to move as the house we were in was in a poor state.

So we moved to Derwent Road in Highfield which was another part of Farnworth and a new chapter began.

The author's Mother

Chapter two

Crying a thousand tears

After receiving the first punch from my father at just four years old, I became very fearful whenever he was around me or in the same room.

I only felt safe around my mother. She was my guardian angel and a shoulder to cry on and she became my rock over the years.

I was always afraid to sleep with the light off so I always made sure it was on. It wasn't just the dark I was afraid of; it was my father who I named the bogeyman for obvious reasons

Every creak or noise in the Middle of the night made me wet myself and put my head under the blankets because I was so afraid.

That one first punch from my dad haunted me and made me have nightmares. As a result, soiling the bed sheets was common practice for me for the next few years.

One particular morning I was having my breakfast with my family and having a laugh like close families should, when I dropped my bowl of cornflakes onto the floor and the bowl smashed. There was a sudden quietness in the room and my father jumped up and slapped me across my face.

I cried out, "I'm sorry it was an accident." I was shaking with fear. I held out my arms to him and he just smirked and walked away. I was just seven years old. I just couldn't understand at the time why he was so horrible to me and why he wanted to punish me.

I remember crying in my room many times and hiding behind the door shaking with fear. I would be too afraid to open the door.

I remember going to school even at the early age of nine years old with small bruises on my face. Frequently I would be crying my eyes out all the way to school as I walked up Derwent Road from my house. It happened many, many times.

The only time I ever felt really safe from him was when I was at school away from his anger and brutality. I lost count of the number of times I cried on my school desk at Our Lady of Lourdes which was an infant school in Farnworth.

I wept till my tears dried up. Concentration was difficult in the class room and I was ticked off by the school teachers on many occasions. I never told them why I was crying and they never asked me why. I was just a mixed up kid who couldn't grasp what was going on. I thought it was normal to be hit by your father.

I do remember some good times, however, with my father but they were few and far between.

I especially looked forward to Christmas Day as most people do. But for me it was very special because all the family was together. On this one special day in the year my father showed his love and never showed any anger. It was a pity that Christmas Day was not every day.

I never slept much the night before, not just because I was afraid of my father coming home drunk but because I was excited about opening my presents.

A typical Christmas Day started when my father came upstairs and told us that Father Christmas had been. He would then take us all down stairs and show us the evidence. There would be a plate with some mince pies and a carrot which had bite marks on it. He used to say, "I heard Father Christmas come down the chimney. He left the presents, had a bite of the mince pies and took the carrots for the reindeers on the way out."

The same person who used to bully me acted the part of Father Christmas by mimicking him with, "Ho, ho, merry Christmas to one and all."

I was so excited I couldn't wait to open my presents. They were in piles for each of us on chairs. As we opened our presents my dad would light the fire which was soon ablaze and we used to throw all the wrapping on the fire.

My mother would be getting the breakfast ready. As for my father; he was loving and caring and he was so excited, watching us opening our presents. I lost count of the number of times I thanked him and in return he would cuddle me. This made me very happy as it was all I ever wanted from him, to hold me and make me feel loved and wanted. Alas, this was just for one day a year.

My mother would cook a special breakfast on Christmas Day. We had all the trimmings; eggs, bacon, mushrooms, tomatoes, beans and piles of toast. After breakfast we would all run upstairs and get changed for church. Other families would join us as we all made our way to the church. We all sang Christmas carols, even my father would sing on the way to the church. The church was packed, far more than usual. A lot of people were standing at the back as there wasn't enough space to sit down. All the family sang Christmas carols and my dad used to squeeze my hand and smile at me. I remember praying to God, thanking him for my father loving me and wishing Christmas Day was every day. It wasn't the presents that made me so happy; I just wanted my father to be loving and happy every day.

After church we would make our way home and we were allowed to play out with our friends for a while. However, we had to be back in for three o'clock as our Christmas dinner would be ready.

We all sat round around the table wearing our Christmas hats. My mother and father and brothers and sisters were all there. On the table there was the biggest Turkey I had ever seen. To this day I cannot work out how she got into the oven. The table was full of roasted potatoes; all the vegetables you could think of and yes the dreaded Brussels sprouts which, like everyone else, we all loved to hate. It was happy days pulling the crackers and laughing and joking about the silly jokes inside the crackers. I had to laugh at my dad because he decided to light the Christmas pudding. He would pull out a bottle of brandy and pour it over the pudding. Then he would put a match to it but nothing happened so he would pour some more brandy on.

Eventually, after several attempts he always managed to get a flame and as his head was so near, on more than one occasion, it set fire to his party hat. For a moment there was silence as we did not know how he would react. He broke silence when he burst out laughing so we all in joined in. It was a special day as my mother and father put so much effort into it.

I was so happy I didn't want Christmas Day to end as I knew he would be unpredictable again in the coming days.

The Turkey would become part of our meals for the rest of the week. How many ways could you cook a turkey? I would think to myself.

To this day I still enjoy Christmas as I love the family gatherings and it is something I will carry on till the end of my days and I hope my children will also maintain the tradition.

However, the bad times soon returned.

Even when I went to St Gregory's secondary school at the age of eleven, I cried on my school desk. I cried so much that my eyes were badly swollen and red. I was too afraid to say anything to the teachers as I was frightened my dad would find out. My education certainly suffered because of the bullying and my reports proved this. When he saw them he would give me a back hander, not realising that it was his fault that I was too upset to work properly at school.

I started to stay away from school as his bullying got worse and my education suffered. I would just go wandering off into town or hide in buildings. This was just to keep away from school; anything to hide my tears and bruises from the teachers and my school friends. The time I was having off began to attract the attention of the teachers and the headmaster wrote a letter to my parents.

This didn't stop me running away from home and my mum ringing the police as she was worried. I lost count of the number of times the police brought me home in a police car. In fact I reached foreign shores when I was fourteen. You can read about that later on in the book.

Running away and afraid to go home and crying on my school desk would be a dark and dominant chapter in my early life. And yes I did cry a thousand tears and the bogeyman I nicknamed my father was real. I would find this out to my cost over the years and the nightmares would carry on for a lot longer.

Living In fear of the night

Hiding under the blankets
Holding your sheets so tight
Closing your eyes, pretending to sleep
You hear footsteps
Creeping through the night
Holding your breath
Tears flowing on your pillow
Cringing with fear
Praying he will go away
You hear the clock, tick tock
The footsteps go away
Was it a bad dream?
Was it the Bogeyman?
No it was your father

Chapter Three

Highfield Bound - a new home

In 1966 we finally moved to our new house in Derwent Road, Highfield, Farnworth. It would be the start of a journey I eventually called, 'To the Abyss.'

The twelve years I lived there were not happy ones even though I was close to my mother and my brothers and sisters.

Denise and Diane were much older than me and it wasn't long before they both went their separate ways and moved on in their lives.

I suffered years of physical and mental abuse from my father and my mother also didn't escape his violent attention. Although she suffered she managed to stay strong and kept the family together with her love and caring ways.

On one occasion, however, my mother had had enough of the torment and the abuse so she took me, my two brothers and my sister to Moor Lane Bus Station in Bolton.

She had very little money but begged and cried to a coach driver by telling him that we had to get away from her husband because she was fearful of him.

The coach driver let us on the bus free and the coach took us to Brixham where my sister Denise lived with her husband John. We stayed there for a week and we were all so happy but it didn't last long as my dad came and begged my mum to return home.

So off we went back to Derwent Road, much against my wishes. After that, for a short while he changed, but it didn't last long before he started drinking and gambling again.

The house we lived in was a new house of recent construction. It had a large back garden which was big enough to play football and we did this on many occasions.

It was a three up and two down with a small kitchen, a living room and a small lounge.

I shared my room with my two brothers, Mark and Stephen. My sister Pat had the small box-room.

I decorated my bedroom with posters of my favourite football team Bolton Wanderers, to the annoyance of my brother Mark who was an Everton fan at the time.

Highfield, where we lived, had a few shops and a pub called the Flying Shuttle. There were plenty of fields where we could play before they built houses there.

I started going to a new school called Our Lady of Lourdes. It was a Catholic school and the teachers were very strict.

If I didn't get a good-hiding at home I got some kind of punishment at school where I frequently received the slipper and the ruler on my knuckles.

Times were hard. At the beginning my father worked and my mother did various jobs to keep the home going.

We still visited the jumble sales and when they started to build houses on the playing fields my dad forced me to pinch wood as we couldn't afford coal and if I refused I would get a clip around the ear.

I befriended an Irish bloke who I called Paddy. He would give me the off-cuts from all the wood he never used. I used to carry sacks of it home which for a while which kept my dad happy.

On a Friday we had a special family treat. My mum used to send me to the local chippy with a big bowl for chips and scraps and pea juice.

I felt like Oliver Twist. "Please sir, can I have some more?"

Even at that young age, between eight and nine, I got into all kinds of trouble. I befriended a lad called Alan who sadly died at the young age of fifteen. R.I.P Alan.

We used to pinch coal from a coal yard and take sacks of it home for my dad, with his blessings.

It was then that I first met Sergeant Swann who was our local copper and who would become more and more of a thorn in my flesh, as time went by.

He caught both Alan and me red-handed once. I received a smack behind the head for my troubles. It wasn't the first and wouldn't be the last one I received of him.

He took me home and I faced the wrath of my father who before that, had given me his blessing for the thieving.

I was punished by my dad on many occasions and every day I lived in fear of him.

Many a time I went to school upset and bruised and I would put my head in my arms on my school desk and sob.

I was too afraid to say anything to my friends or teachers in case my dad found out. I was scared of getting another beating.

My dad kept me locked up in my room so I wouldn't get into any trouble with my friends but I used to escape through the box-room window onto the ledge and then run off and play with them.

This carried on for a number of years through my youth; the more he beat me, the more I rebelled.

In 1969 I left Our Lady of Lourdes and went to a secondary school called Saint Gregory's in Farnworth.

Saint Gregory's was not known for having star pupils among the boys at that time and it was a breeding ground for football hooligans who learnt their trade with fist fights on the school playing fields.

It was something I learnt and got involved in, in my later school days.

I hated my first year there. I was only small and most of the boys were a lot bigger than me. The first day I started school, I was chased by all the year eleven boys and I was caught and pushed head first into a school bin. This was an initiation test for all new-comers.

This carried on for the first few days and I was getting scared and fed up with it so one day a lad who I won't name, he was 15 at the time and a lot bigger than me, tried to put me in one of the school bins. I started to stick up for myself and I hit him so hard I knocked him over the school bin.

He started to cry and he ran off to a school teacher, the infamous Mr Eckersley. He came over to me and grabbed my ear and took me in to his office.

I tried to explain what had gone on but he wouldn't have any of it. I was forced to stay behind on detention and do five hundred lines after school. I should have finished school at 3.45 but it was now 4.30. I was getting very worried and frightened by the prospect of facing my father.

I made my way through the school gates and I was confronted by the same lad I had earlier knocked over the school bin. He was not alone. He had four school friends with him who were all a lot older and bigger than me.

I was punched and kicked on to the floor and I was screaming out with pain. It was only the intervention of a member of the public that stopped me getting a severe beating.

My face was badly bruised and my nose was bleeding and my school jumper was ripped. I was now frightened of going home and facing the wrath of my father.

I took my time getting back and when I approached my house my legs went like jelly. I knocked on the door and my mother opened it. I told her what happened and she took me upstairs and cleaned me up.

I never saw my dad till the morning and when I did he slapped me across the face and said, "That's for losing and next time if you come home like that you will get a bigger hiding from me."

I didn't finish my breakfast. I kissed my mum good bye and walked to school. When I was in view of the school gates I could see the lads who had beaten me.

I stopped but they saw me and they started to run towards me. It was then that I ran like a bat from hell; they chased me for what seemed like ages.

I decided there and then that I wasn't going back to school and didn't go for months at a time.

I used to pretend to my mum that I was going every morning and instead I just went for walks in the town centre. Eventually all this came to an end as the headmaster complained by letter to my parents and I was threatened that if it carried on, I would be expelled from school.

After a good lecture from my mother and the usual beating from my father, I thought it would be wiser to face all my problems at school.

My two brothers and I were becoming the school joke because of our haircuts. They used to call us the Beatles because we all had the same haircuts. My mum used to cut our hair with a pudding-basin - thanks mum!

The first year soon passed and I was now into my second year. I was now twelve years old and the bullying stopped. I started to fight back and I started to gain a bit of respect from my school mates.

If I didn't get a black eye at school anymore I would get one from my dad when he lost in his gambling.

During the next few years, however, I was getting into more and more scrapes at school, fighting for my family honour and fights against other schools and the strap and the cane were common experiences for me.

I didn't need an appointment with the headmaster. I would just knock on his door and he would say, "Come in Ian. I was expecting you."

The sound of my cries

I would wake up crying
I held out my arms
To be held and to be loved
Bad dreams of my father
I felt the hand of my father
Nightmares returned with a vengeance
Long and lonely nights
I cried a thousand tears
Nightmares and fears

The sound of my cries
Echoed through the night
Alone and afraid
I longed to be loved
The clock was ticking
Through the quiet night
I heard the footsteps coming
I knew my father was coming
I shut my eyes, hoping he would go away
I lay in the darkness quaking
Praying he would go away

The sound of my cries
Echoed through the night
The door opened, I opened my eyes
It was my mother, she held me so tightly
Wiping away the tears on my cheeks
She would rock me to sleep
She kissed my cheek, good night my love
I fell asleep

Chapter four

Knock on the door and run!

Some of the things I used to get up to when I was young make me chuckle now.

I remember at nine years old an old school friend, John and I went to the same school together and we used to harass the neighbours by knocking repeatedly on their front-doors and then running away. We did this on a regular occasion and we became so infamous that the neighbours would complain frequently to my parents to the annoyance of my father. He would then give me a back-hander for my trouble.

I was always getting into mischief, but it all seemed like good fun at the time.

I remember on one occasion Alan and I, he was my best mate at the time, knocked on this particular house on Anchor Lane, near my home. It was seven on a winter's evening and it was dark. All the lights were on in the house and most of the curtains where drawn. Alan and I, giggling like most nine year olds do, knocked on the front door and there was no answer. So I told Alan let's knock on the front window and keep knocking till someone answers the door. We seemed to be knocking on the window and door for a good few minutes and it seemed like ages. However, we persisted. We both should have walked away and knocked on the next door but we didn't. Suddenly the door opened and out came a man; he was very angry and shouting obscenities at us both. He was huge, in his late thirties and in a terrible rage. He got hold of me and slapped me across the face. He then kicked me on the shins and as I was rolling on the floor in agony, he then turned his attention to

Alan who was terrified and frozen to the spot. He gave him a slap across the back of head and then grabbed him pushed him against the wall shouting at the top of his voice that if we every knocked on his door again we would get the same treatment.

We both hobbled away but not before we gave him the 'wankers' sign. I looked a sorry state with my face bruised on one side and my right leg also badly bruised and swollen. I looked at Alan and he was visibly shaken by the experience.

I told Alan that if our parents asked any questions about our bruises that we should say that we had had a fight with each other but we made friends again straight afterwards.

I sat Alan down on a wall near the Flying Shuttle, a pub which I would patronise in my older days. I told Alan who was sobbing that we would get our revenge so not to worry. We planned our next visit would be on Guy Fawkes Night.

I called for Alan at 7.30 as arranged. I knocked on his front door and his father answered. I was told Alan was not playing out as he was ill, so I walked away huffing and puffing and calling Alan all the names under the sun. I decided to carry through my plan of action on my own and went to the paper shop at the top of the road. I knew the shop owner who was called Mr Flanagan and he was a close friend of my family. Also he had a son who I disliked for various reasons and went to the same school as me. Anyway, I ordered a box of bangers and three rockets with the small amount of pocket money I had saved up. I then headed for the Flying Shuttle which was surrounded by a small brick wall but most importantly it was facing the house of the man who had given Alan and me a hard time. The Flying Shuttle was next to Anchor Lane so it was easy to conceal myself by hiding behind the wall. I found a small bottle and put one of the rockets in it and aimed at the man's window. I lit the rocket and 'whoosh' it just missed his window. I had two rockets left so I aimed the rocket with more accuracy and then I lit the second rocket. 'Whoosh' off it went but this time it hit his window with a loud bang. I peeped over the wall and the bloke in question came out. I was giggling as I could see him waving his hands about in anger. I then lit my third and final rocket and aimed at his window again and 'whoosh' it hit his window again. The man then came running out and checked his window and I could see him waving his hands around in anger again. I was giggling and I muttered and clenched my fist and said, "yeah."

The man was very angry and looked towards where the rocket could have come from and started to head in my direction. It was time to run so I headed towards the shops and kept well out of his sight.

However, I hadn't finished with him. I still had a box of bangers to put through his letter box. I waited for an hour or so before I went back as I didn't fancy facing his wrath.

I walked over to the Flying Shuttle and hid behind the wall facing his house. It was now 8.30 pm. I was late going back home as I should have been home for half past seven and I knew I was going to be in trouble with my parents; especially my father. There was only one light on in the man's house and that was in an upstairs window. I headed toward his place again and checked to make sure no one was hanging around and I sneaked towards his front door. I lit all the box of bangers waited a few seconds then lifted up his letter box and threw them in. Then I ran like a bat out of hell. I heard a loud bang and it echoed through the

30

night and I ran off laughing, mission completed I had my ultimate revenge.

My hatred for this man didn't just stop there. I would carry on harassing him for the next few years. After all, I was just a skinny nine years old and he was a mature man and had been completely out of order in assaulting two young kids so viciously.

I went back home and I faced the wrath of my father yet again, but it was well worth it and I still chuckle about it to this day.

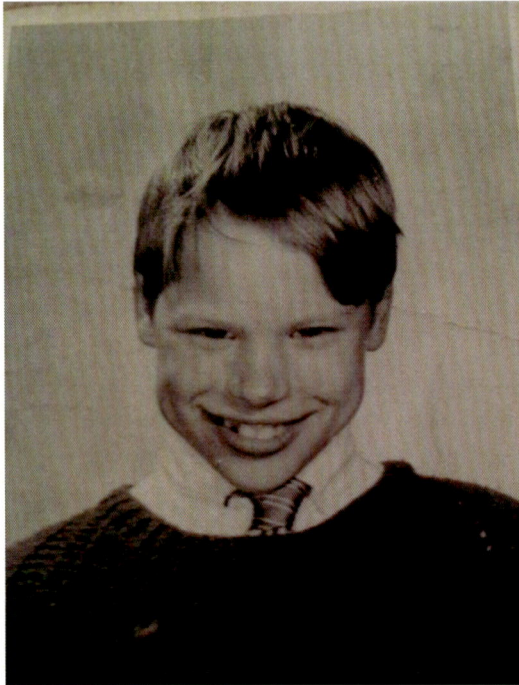

The author at 10 years old

Chapter five

The Infamous Sergeant Swann

Sergeant Swann was as tough as they come he was six foot tall and about twenty stone to match. He lived just at the top of my road in one of the police houses. Over the years he would become a thorn in my side.

I crossed his path many times. It started from a young age and many times I would receive a clout behind the ear and be dragged to my mother's house where I would receive another good hiding from my dad for getting caught.

The first time our paths crossed was outside the shops. I was only nine years old. The shops were at the top of the road where I lived at the time. There was a newspaper shop a chip-shop and a post office and there was also a small Co-op mini-mart which was rich pickings for me and my school friends. We would fill our pockets with sweets on our way to school and as we got older and more daring would put bottles of cider under our jackets.

Anyway, I was with a number of my friends playing football when I kicked the ball and knocked the Sergeant's helmet off. He went red in face and I could see he was getting increasingly angry that we were all laughing at him. It was like a red rag to a bull and he came storming over and clipped me round my ear and said, "You are not laughing now, are you?" He took our ball from us and just walked away laughing.

The second occasion when our paths crossed was when I and number of friends were caught pinching toffees from the penny tray. The owner of the shop reported us to police and we were held in the store room like criminals. I was 'shitting' myself and when the door opened and I saw Sergeant Swann he commented, "Well, well, well, who do we have here? It's our local Fagin and his little gang."

He took all our names and he wasn't happy to see me but he just smirked and told us to leave the shop. He told me specially that he would be making a visit to my house.

I started to worry what would my father do if he found out but for some reason the knock on my door never came.

I was getting into trouble now on what seemed to be a weekly basis for what seemed like trivial things; playing football, knocking on a door and running away and for just being a nuisance with the public.

It was always Sergeant Swann on the warpath. Once I was caught stealing coal from one of my neighbour's coal bunkers with my dad's blessing and received a good hiding from my dad for getting caught by the infamous Police Sergeant.

When I was thirteen years old, my four friends and I; I won't name as I don't want to embarrass them, stole three bottles cider from the paper shop.

We were all drinking it on the steps at the back of the Flying Shuttle which was our local pub. At the time the Flying Shuttle was infamous for its pub brawls. It was wrecked on many occasions and was only patronised by the local idiots.

Anyway, we were all getting drunk on the cider and having a laugh, making a nuisance of ourselves. It wasn't long before we came to the attention of Sergeant Swann. I don't know how he found us but somebody must have tipped him off. He came over to us with his usual sarcastic grin. I have to admit I was 'shitting' myself, my legs were like jelly. He took the bottles from us and put them in a plastic bag to throw them in the bin. He took all our names, as usual, but this time he held me and told the rest of my friends to go home and said he would be making a visit to their parents. As they walked away he snarled at me and grabbed me by the ear and dragged me to my house which was only a few minutes away. Along the way he kept telling me I was a pain in the backside and he was sick of me and that I was a problem to society.

I was at the door of my house and my stomach was doing summersaults. My legs were like jelly at the prospect of facing my dad.

Sergeant Swann knocked on door and to my shock my dad opened the door. Before I could speak sergeant Swann told my dad that I had been drinking cider and making a nuisance of myself (true) and making obscene gestures at the public (a lie.)

He tried to give the impression to my dad that we had stolen the cider from the local co-op but he couldn't prove it

My dad told him he will sort me out and that I wouldn't be playing out for a very long time. This brought a huge smile to the Sergeant's face.

My dad dragged me through the door and punched me a few times and told me to go to my room and stay there.

I was glad I wasn't going to school as it was holiday time and I was sick of going with bruises on my face.

For the next few days I never went out and I only came down stairs to eat my meals.

My mum told me to start behaving myself and that I wasn't helping myself with my dad.

One day my mother received some bad news which rocked the whole family. My dad's mum who we called little nanny, had died. We all loved her very much. She had lived with us for a long time and mum used to look after her as she had had both legs amputated.

My dad was heartbroken on the day of the funeral. For whatever reason he took his upset out on me and punched me in the face and blacked my eye.

I was shaking with fear and I was crying my eyes out. Only the intervention of my mother saved me from more punishment.

After the funeral I was determined to run away to France and my decision was made.

Back to sergeant Swann I wanted to get my own back on him so I had a plan of action. I bought a black spray from the local garage and I was going to put graffiti on the front of his house and get my ultimate revenge.

So, one night I sneaked out of the box-room window, which I had used for my escape, many times in the past.

I made my way up the road to Sergeant Swann's house. It was three o'clock in the morning. I sneaked up his path; made sure everybody was in bed and that there were no lights on in the house. Then I sprayed in big black letters 'Mini BWFC' which I would use as my status many times in local football grounds over the years.

I also sprayed, 'Sergeant Swann is a fat bastard,' in huge letters across the front of his house.

The job was now done and it was time to disappear. I made my way back to my house with a huge smile on my face I climbed up the drain pipe and through the window and sneaked into my bed with huge satisfaction on my face. Revenge was sweet, I said to myself.

A few days later I was walking up Derwent road with my mum when Sergeant Swann spotted us. He came running over to us. He was gesturing as he approached us.

He was going crazy shouting, "I know it was you who vandalised my house and if I could prove it I would arrest you and have you charged."

My mum went berserk with him and accused him of harassing me and that she would report him. He marched off waving his arms and muttering under his breath. I had a huge smile on my face and I was so happy to get my ultimate revenge.

I kept a low profile after that and I tried to avoid him whenever possible.

Our paths did cross a few times over the next few years, however. The last time was on a field next to Anchor Lane in Highfield where I lived. It was a road which led to a flyover bridge into Little Hulton.

There were a good thirty lads from Highfield and we were having a bit of a stand-off with our hated enemies from Little Hulton the Spillymies.

There were over sixty lads from both sides having a free-for-all. Bottles and bricks were being thrown and some lads were carrying knives.

Then in the background we heard the police sirens and knew it was time to leave. The cavalry had arrived and they came armed with police batons and police dogs. It was time to run for our lives. I and another lad who I'll just call Liam ran through someone's garden.

Then we heard this loud voice shout my name and I turned around to see Sergeant Swann. He was threatening us both with arrest. He was knackered, red in the face and gasping for breath. Me and Liam just stopped and laughed at him and shouted, "You fat bastard don't you think you need to retire now? You're passed it and so over-weight."

We just couldn't stop laughing as we trotted off. He was too exhausted to catch us.

That was the last time I crossed paths with Sergeant Swann. I did see him on various occasions later on and I couldn't resist muttering a few obscenities whenever I saw him.

He sadly died after I had moved away from Highfield. I never held any malice towards him. After all he was only doing his job and he was probably a decent bloke underneath that uniform.

R.I.P. Sergeant Swann. Thanks for all the fun we used to have together. I still chuckle to this day when I think about it.

Chapter six

Catholic boy

As a good catholic boy I was religiously dragged to church every Sunday. My earliest recollection of the faith was saying my prayers at the dinner table, which my dad always insisted on before we could eat our meals.

It was only when I went to Our Lady of Lourdes that the true meaning of being a catholic was fully explained to me.

I do remember in my naive innocence I used to pray to God asking him to protect me from my father; of course my prayers were never answered.

I used to enjoy going to Our Lady of Lourdes. We used to do nativity plays at Christmas. I always used to play the part of an angel. Going to church with the school became a pleasure. I really enjoyed singing in the choir especially at Christmas and Easter and not just because of gifts I used to receive, but because of the warmth and the good feeling. They made feel part of an extended family and it made it harder for me when I had to go back home because of the beatings from my father.

It was at this time that I started to ask my dad question about being a good catholic. I remember asking him if it wasn't a sin to steal wood from building sites and also to steal coal. My dad's response was swift; a good clip round side of my head. "It's a sin when you don't do as you are told by your father," he replied.

It was then that religion became confusing. It was around this time that I had started to go to classes for my Confirmation. Confirmation, a sacrament of initiation, establishes young adults as fully-fledged members of the faith. This sacrament was called *Confirmation* because the faith given in Baptism was now confirmed and made strong. During your Baptism, your parents and godparents make promises to renounce Satan and believe in God and the Church on your behalf. At Confirmation, you renew these same promises, this time speaking for yourself.

During Confirmation, the focus is on the Holy Spirit, who confirmed the Apostles on Pentecost and gave them courage to practice their faith. Catholics believe that the same Holy Spirit confirms Catholics during the Sacrament of Confirmation and gives them the same gifts.

Traditionally, the seven *gifts* of the Holy Spirit are wisdom, understanding, counsel, fortitude (courage), knowledge, piety, and fear of the Lord. These gifts are supernatural graces given to the soul. The twelve *fruits* of the Holy Spirit are charity, joy, peace, patience, benignity, goodness, long-suffering, mildness, faith, modesty, continency and chastity — human qualities

I remember the day well. I felt I was the best dressed there and I really was the part. I was wearing a white shirt and a tie and black pants with a brand new pair of shiny black shoes. My mum did me really proud that day. All the girls wore white dresses and after we were confirmed we did our walk around the parish. I felt really proud that I was part of the catholic family and so were my family and friends.

Shortly after that I went to my first confession. I think it was a Thursday night. I had to go into a side room in the church. Then I had to kneel down in front of a small window-like opening with a fine mesh over it. I think the idea was I couldn't see the priest but I could hear him. I was already informed beforehand what to expect from the priest and what to say.

I can't remember if he spoke first but I remember blurting out, "forgive me father, I have sinned. While I was playing football today I knocked a policeman's helmet off and I stole some toffees from the penny tray." I swear I heard a slight chuckle followed by, "I want you to ask forgiveness and say three Hail Mary's."

The following day we all compared notes at school on our confessions.

What was to follow was something of a competition between all my school friends as to who would say the most Hail Mary's. Please remember we were still very young and just learning the faith.

My father would give all my brothers and sisters money for the collection when we went to church every Sunday morning. Whilst in church I used to say a little prayer. "Please forgive me God for keeping the collection money." I used it buy sweets at the corner shop on Plodder Lane on the way home.

As I started to get older, I got more frustrated with the teachings of my faith as my father would only beat me for stealing when I got caught. I was utterly confused as I was always taught by the church that stealing was a sin.

My dad always claimed to be a good catholic because I always thought he confessed his sins. I know now his actions were just an excuse and nothing to do with religion.

I started to skip going to church as I lost faith because of my father's actions. The way he treated me and my mother, and he had the nerve to say he was a good catholic.

Many times my mother would catch me skipping church. She always told me what colour the priest's vestments were. As some Sunday's he would wear a different colour vestments. She knew my father would ask me questions to see if I had been to church.

I got to know the priest very well. His name was Father Melvin. He was a very nice genuine person who I know often advised my mother to leave my father. On the odd occasion, Father Melvin would point out strongly that I had not been seen in church and what was the last time I had been to confession? I would reply with my fingers crossed behind my back that I had been a good boy, Father. I tried not to smile too much when I said this.

I may not attend church but I am still a good catholic at heart. I still tell my children to attend church and I hope unlike me they will always stay on the right path.

Chapter seven

Paris, freedom but all alone

When I was fourteen I decided enough was enough. I was fed up with the constant bullying from my dad. I wanted to be free and out of his clutches.

I had already saved up a bit of money and took more out of my dad's wallet every time he came home drunk. I had a total of thirty pounds. That was a lot of money in those days. I had a small rucksack to put a few bits of clothing and some food and drink into.

I had always wanted to go to France and Paris was the destination I chose. Now I had to have a plan of action and find out how I would travel there. I already knew I could get a sixty hour excursion document from the ferry company as long I signed it as though I was 16 and as long as they were satisfied that I would be back in England before the 60 hours expired. Little did they know I had no intention of returning to England?

I planned to leave on the Saturday, in the early hours; all I had to do now was to try to stay out of my dad's way and keep out trouble.

I had tried to act normally with my mother but every time she smiled at me I felt like breaking down.

I had never been separated from my mother before and I felt very sad that I was running away but I had to go. I loved my mother so much and I felt like I was abandoning her.

I couldn't take the beatings any longer and being locked away from my friends.

I kissed her good night and hugged her very tight. I told her that I loved her very much and off I went to bed. I had to stay awake as I knew I was leaving in the early hours. I cried so much through the night as I just couldn't stop thinking about my mother.

But my mind was already made up. In the early hours of the morning I packed my rucksack with a few clothes and essentials and sneaked out of the box-room window once again. I jumped onto the ledge and then climbed down the drain pipe.

I looked at my mum's bedroom and my tears started to run down the side of my face. I turned around and I ran up Derwent Road like a bat from hell.

It was 5.30 in the morning and I had to find my way into Bolton and get there as quickly as possible before my mother found me missing.

I walked it to Bolton which was only a forty minute walk and I made my way to Moor Lane which was our main bus and coach station.

I had already booked a coach to London Victoria station but it wasn't leaving until seven o'clock so I just waited the half hour sitting on a bench and deep in thought.

The half hour passed very quickly and it wasn't long before the coach for London Victoria arrived.

There weren't many people waiting and they were mainly old. The coach door opened and it was here that my adventure began. I climbed into the coach and showed my ticket to the driver. He just looked at me and nodded his head.

I went straight to the back of the coach and sat next to the window as the coach started to pull out of the bus station.

I suddenly felt all alone and I didn't want to think what lay ahead for me but I didn't feel afraid. I just felt relieved that I was finally free; free from fear and the hand of my father.

It wasn't long before we were on the motorway and Bolton was now a distant memory. I was heading for Paris on an adventure and a journey into the unknown.

I fell asleep and I slept nearly all the way and that was six hours solid.

We arrived in London on time and now I had to find where the coach was to Dover.

I found that I didn't need to ask strangers where the ticket office was. People were continually asking me if I was lost and if I was alright. I was only small for my age with a baby-face. This was becoming a hindrance no matter where I went.

Victoria Coach Station is the largest coach station in London. It serves long-distance coach services and is also the departure point for many countrywide coach tours originating from London.

I made my way across the station to where the ticket office was. For the first time I noticed people begging which I had never seen before and people sleeping rough. Little did I know this would be the world I would be living in? I quickly purchased the ticket for Dover.

The trip to Dover was uneventful. It felt just as long as the journey from Bolton but it only took a few hours.

I purchased my ticket with much difficulty at the ferry-office. Not having a passport I needed a special permit for a short visit to France. I had to convince the guy at the ticket office that my mother lived in Paris, and I was sixteen years old. When he started to question my story I burst into tears.

I was so scared of being caught at this point but to my relief he gave me the pass.

I didn't have to wait long before I was boarding the ferry to Calais. I changed what little money I had into French Francs.

I looked into my rucksack and 'the cupboard was almost bare.' I ate and drank what was left. I then made my way to the top deck. I could just make out the white cliffs of Dover disappearing into the distance behind me. It was then that I started to cry uncontrollably. My feelings were all confused. Even though I was free from my father's abuse I couldn't help feeling sad that I was abandoning my mother.

I don't know how long I was crying but the famous white cliffs of Dover were now beginning to fade completely from my view. The ship was sailing for Calais. A new adventure lay ahead. It could only be better than the life I had left behind.

The ship docked at Calais. I was now free but alone. I made my way to the train station where I purchased my ticket to Paris.

I was soon to realise how naive I was because most French people didn't speak any English. I realised this all the more when I arrived in Paris.

The journey from Calais to Paris was long and boring as it was night-time and you couldn't see much in the darkness.

I slept most of the journey away and I was awakened by a guard on the train who tried to explain that I was now in Paris.

I wiped my eyes and nodded my head in a gesture of understanding and made my way off the train and just followed the crowd out of the station.

By now it was dark but still quite warm even though it was in the early hours and the crowds from the train started to disappear.

I decided that it was time to find somewhere I could sleep; where it was safe from prying eyes.

I started to walk up the nearest street I could find. I remember noticing the houses were different from the ones I grew up with. They were huge and colourful and I noticed the windows were different; some of them looked like doors and the streets were narrow.

I noticed a large wagon covered with a green canvas cover just parked up. I lifted the canvas and peered in. Inside there were some articles of furniture and a few bits of carpet and cushions. They looked soft and inviting and I was so tired I soon fell asleep.

I awoke with the hustle and bustle as Paris began to wake up. For a second I did not know where I was until I heard people speaking French.

I peered out the wagon to see if it was clear to jump out. It was and I started walking. By this time I was hungry and thirsty. I could smell freshly baked bread so I followed my nose to a small bakery. The shop window display was full of different kinds of shaped breads.

I went inside and I noticed a man who was huge in size and had a large beard. I tapped him on the arm and asked him for a ham buttie.

He spoke in French and gestured to me, obviously he didn't understand what I was saying.

So I pointed to some bread and ham and cheese and a bottle of water. I then showed him the amount of money I had left in my hand.

He shrugged his shoulders and made me the biggest ham and cheese sandwich I had ever seen. I thought it would last me all week.

The guy took every cent I had but I think now I got the better end of the deal as I suspect he took pity on me.

I stepped out of the shop and waved goodbye. I sat down on a bench tucking in to my ham and cheese buttie, watching the world go by.

I noticed tables and chairs on the pavement and people arriving drinking coffee. I found it strange but fascinating.

I wanted to see the Eiffel Tower which was supposed to be miles bigger then our Blackpool tower. I just started to walk. I don't know how long I was walking for but it seemed to be forever.

I asked passers bye and I tried to say Eiffel Tower. Most just walked past and shrugged their shoulders.

Eventually an elderly English couple took pity on me. They asked me why I was on my own. I told them that I had lost my parents and that I had no money and I was supposed to be meeting them at the Eiffel Tower.

I put on the waterworks and it worked. They gave me ten Francs and they took me to a bus-stop so that I could get a bus to the Eiffel Tower.

It wasn't long before a small bus arrived and I just followed the few tourists onto the bus. I was only small so I was able to sneak on the bus undetected and I made my way to the back.

The journey to the centre of Paris didn't take long. I was in awe of the beautiful buildings and the architecture and I could see the Eiffel Tower in the distance.

When the bus arrived at the destination I just followed the crowds. I was overwhelmed by the sheer size of all the structures.

There were hundreds of cafés with tables outside and all the tables were full of people eating and drinking coffee.

You could smell the local pastries and garlic. By now I was getting hungry and thirsty. I was in my second day in

Paris and I had very little money; all I had left was a few francs.

I went to one of the little shops in the square and all I could afford was a bottle of water. The shop was pretty full so I had to decide pretty quickly. If I wanted to survive I needed food.

I opened my small jacket and put a couple of small loafs and some pieces of cheese under my arm. Then I made my way to the counter and paid for the bottle of water with the small change I had.

My heart was pounding and I was fearful of getting caught but to my surprise the shop owner just smiled at me.

I made my way out of his small shop with a massive grin on my face. I decided that I had to eat now as I was starving and thirsty as the heat of the day was scorchingly hot.

I sat down on and while I was eating I was looking at the thousands of tourist just walking about. They all spoke different languages as they came from all over the world.

I could see the Eiffel Tower in the distance. This was my next plan of action; I had to see one of the main attractions of Europe. I followed the crowds and headed for the Eiffel Tower. The walk would take me past museums and fancy shops and there were plenty of restaurants.

When I arrived at the huge Eiffel Tower there were literally thousands of people in large queues. I sat on the grass bank. I was just amazed at the beauty and splendour of Paris and its surroundings. I just laughed to myself as I thought how different it was to where I lived in Highfield.

It was getting on now; nearly 9 pm in the evening and I was getting thirsty and hungry again.

I also had to find somewhere to sleep, so I was on the lookout for wagons that were parked up.

I headed for the narrow streets and away from the hustle and bustle of the crowds. I could smell the hot pastries and the smell of fresh bread was everywhere I went.

I passed what looked like apartment blocks and outside one of them was a large truck covered in blue canvass. I looked inside and it was empty so I decided to bed down there for the night.

I was tired and exhausted and I was still hungry and thirsty. I must have fallen asleep pretty quickly as I was awoken by the sound of traffic and the noise of passing people.

I peeped through the canvas and when it was all clear I jumped out and made my way up the narrow streets.

I passed a bakery and outside there were bread and pastries on trolleys. It was my chance to feed myself. I took what I could and disappeared before I got caught.

I headed for the embankment along the river Seine. I walked for miles and every now and again I would stop and watch the floating restaurants and tourist boats.

There were plenty of cafés and restaurants along the embankment. There were also hundreds of artist painting the scenic views.

I sat and watched them painting for a while. The heat of the day was scorching and I was very thirsty.

I was getting desperate. I needed water and food pretty quickly. I sat next to the embankment and I started begging.

People looked at me and just passed me by. I had to take desperate measures. I picked myself up and did something that was alien to me.

I tried to be a pickpocket and to steal out of people's handbags while they were busy looking at the shops and admiring the sights of Paris.

I wasn't getting anywhere. I was feeling sick with the hunger and thirst. It was now my third day in Paris and I was feeling alone, desperate and very weak.

I tried again to pick pockets but I was useless. Out of the corner of my eye I saw three black youths coming towards me. Before I could I make a decision they were on me like pack of wolves. They slapped me across my face and grabbed me by the throat. I was shaking with fear. They were shouting at me in French and they threw my bag over the embankment and ran off.

I quickly realised that I must have been on their patch. I hastily walked away along the embankment with tears rolling down my face. My thoughts were now about my mother and my family but I was scared to go home and face the wrath of my father.

I was alone and frightened. I didn't know where to turn next; I was hungry and thirsty and very weak. I thought I was going to die. I was just desperate for food and water so I just walked straight into a shop and grabbed a bottle of water. It was then that I heard a loud voice in French. I turned around and it was all over. The shopkeeper grabbed me and took me into the backroom. He sat me down and I just looked at him. I was too weak to say anything.

He left the room and I put my head in my hands and I wept. I was interrupted by a hand on my shoulder. I looked up with my tired eyes to see two French police officers.

They told me in broken English to follow them as I was being taken to the police station.

As I passed the shop keeper he just smiled at me. He must have taken pity on me.

I arrived at the police-station in a police car. I put my head on the window and I just wept. I was tired and weak.

In the police station one of the officers rubbed my hair and then held my hand and took me further into the building.

I found myself in a small room with just a table and chairs. They left the room and after a short while an English speaking officer came in.

He asked me how old I was. I told him I was fourteen. He then asked me why I was here in Paris and how did I get here.

I told him I had run away from home because I wasn't getting on with my father. He then replied that I was lucky not to be charged as I was under age.

While I was talking to him another police officer came in with a bottle of coke and a ham sandwich. I was then told that after I had eaten and cleaned myself up I would be taken to the British Embassy and they would make the necessary arrangements to get me home.

It was a short journey across Paris and I was now sight-seeing in comfort but I knew my adventure was coming to an end.

I had a smile on my face I had probably done what most children wouldn't do in a lifetime and I felt proud of that.

I had done things alien to me in desperation to survive but I was glad now it was coming to end. I was happy that I was going back home to be near my family and at this time I didn't care about facing the wrath of my father.

I arrived at the Embassy and I was met by an Embassy official. He took me inside the building and showed me a room with a bed in it. He then told me I would be sleeping there for the night and that I would be going home to England in the morning.

I was taken into a room and he asked me lots of questions; why I came to Paris and how did I get there? I just smiled and replied I always fancied coming to Paris and that I had a bet at school with my friends.

I lied to him as I knew I would be going home to my family and I didn't want them asking any questions about my father.

He just smiled and said it was time to ring my parents and he asked me what the number was? He gave me a piece of paper and I wrote the number down.

The embassy official then telephoned my mother and spoke to her. "We have your son," he informed her.

"Why? Where is he?" my bewildered mother asked.

"He's in Paris."

There was silence before I heard my mother exclaim, "Paris? I'll bloody kill him when he gets home!" Looking back, it seems I was never afraid of striking out on my own to find pastures new.

I don't remember much about the trip home. I know I travelled by coach and ferry. When I finally got home my mother was waiting for me.

I knocked on the door and my mother opened it. She burst out crying and held me in her arms. She told me that the police had been looking for me and that they had searched the house and even the attic.

She held me and made me promise that I wouldn't run away again. I cried in her arms and said I was sorry.

That was the end of one journey and little did I know that a few years later I would be going on another one that would turn out to be a bigger nightmare and one I certainly wouldn't forget.

Motherly love

I cried for you
Mother
Sailing across the English Channel
All alone and afraid at fourteen
Running away from beatings and fears
I cried a thousand tears
Dad why oh why, do you hurt me?
Sailing across the deep blue sea
I waved good bye to the white cliffs of Dover
I longed for my mother's embrace
I cried for you
Mother

Paris

I arrived on foreign shores
Lost and alone
Afraid and fearful
Strange buildings, funny windows
Strange people, strange words.

Mother I miss you
Mother I need you
Strange inviting smells
Hungry and cold
All alone

Mother I miss you

Eiffel Tower, boats on the river Seine
Strange people, strange words
Free from the fists of my father
Fourteen and all alone

Mother I miss you
Afraid to go home
Fists are all that await me
Scared, hungry and afraid
Desperate and alone
I stole food and water to survive
Alleyways where I slept
Tears were my lullaby

Mother I miss you
I cried myself to sleep
I cried a thousand tears
Paris, thousands of people
All alone and afraid
All I wanted was love from my father
All that' awaits me is fists and tears
I cried a thousand tears

Mother I miss you
Please God make my father love me.
Caught by the police
Time to go home
I pray that I will be safe
All I want is to be held and to be loved

Chapter eight

Back to school and a hero

After my adventure in France it was back to normality. I had return to school. I was in the fourth year and getting up to all kinds of mischief.

It was my first day back at school after the summer holidays and my adventures in Paris.

In the class room all my friends were shaking my hand and congratulating me on finding my way to Paris. Even some of the teachers were happy to see me and they were telling me that they were amazed that I had travelled so far without being caught by the police.

I was totally overwhelmed by the reception I received. I suddenly felt six foot tall and I had a big to smile to match. However, the big smile didn't last long as I bumped into the deputy headmaster, Mr Ekersley, in the hallway.

He made it pretty clear to me that I was no hero but an embarrassment to the school and that he would be watching my activities at school with close scrutiny.

I crossed his path many times through my school days, right up to the last day when I left school.

The first time I felt his wrath had been when I was smoking behind the bike sheds which I did during the school breaks. He came over to me and gave his usual clap-trap to which I replied, "Sod off."

His response was to slap me so hard across my cheek that, to the shock of my school friends, I fell over the bin. I then ran off to the toilet crying and washed my face.

His actions resulted in my mum coming to school the following morning to put a formal complaint in and receiving a humble apology from Mr Ekersley.

I lost count of the number of times I received the strap and the cane from him. He used to save me till he had dealt with all the other offenders and he would have a big grin on his face. I was never away from his office and I didn't need an appointment. I would just knock on his door and he would say, "Come in Ian, I was expecting you."

I did get my little revenges on him now and again. I used to put drawing pins on his chair. On one occasion I threw a stink bomb through his window and I even sent him a personalised letter calling him a 'wanker.' I signed it to say it came from his one and only hated number one pupil.

He used to have his own trade-mark. He had studs under his shoes so you could hear him coming a mile off as he walked down the school corridors. Everybody used to stand to attention when he walked past. I never did, much to his annoyance.

I started to get a name for myself at school, on and off the field. I was involved in fights with other schools especially St James.

I remember on one occasion a good hundred of us from school, from nearly every year, were armed with sticks and all kinds of weapons as we made our way to St James.

We chased hundreds of them down a hill along with some of their teachers.

The police came and chased us all through the estates, quite a few were caught but I was lucky and I got away.

I used to dread my school reports and taking them home as I knew my dad would be angry with my poor grades. He always told me that I was as thick as a barge-pole and he would follow it up with a crack to the back of my head.

I was always late home because I was perpetually on detention and many a time I would go home with a black eye. When that happened, my dad used to say to me, "Did you win?" And if I replied, "No," I would get another crack for losing.

I was always getting up to mischief at school. I remember on one occasion we were supposed to be running in a school marathon around Farnworth but a handful of us caught the bus. However, we were all caught getting off the bus by Mr Walsh, one off our school teachers. He wasn't amused at our escapade and we had to apologise to the whole school in the school assembly hall.

I was punished many times. I had the strap, the cane; I even had a blackboard duster thrown at my head. I had the slipper and a ruler across my knuckles and then lines in detention. That was the only time I ever learned any English.

As for girls I never really fancied anybody at school except one girl who had massive boobs. I won't name her but if she ever reads my book I think she will know who I'm talking about.

I received my first kiss from a girl called Carol. She didn't go to my school; she went to my arch-enemies St James and it was over before it started.

My first sexual experience was with a girl called Susan. I was fourteen at the time and very immature and I wasn't sexually experienced at all. She was twenty-one years old.

I had met her through a friend of mine and she invited me one day to her flat. I made sure I had a few beers to calm my nerves before I met up with her.

She had long blonde hair and ample breasts and she was much taller than me. I knocked on her door and Susan opened it. She was wearing a very low red top over her blue jeans.

She looked very sexy and it wasn't long before we had sex but it was over before it started. This was the first time and the only time I ever had sex with her as I never heard of her again and it was quite obvious I was a let-down to her.

I had a few girl friends but nothing to write home about. I carried on being a rogue at school and education was the least of my worries.

I wasn't happy at home and I just wanted to have fun and a laugh with friends and to go off fighting kids from other schools. That was all part of the fun.

I started to get involved in football hooliganism at an early age. I started to go to Burnden Park which was the home of Bolton Wanderers, with some of my school friends. There was always trouble there, every week.

The first trouble I saw was against Manchester City in an evening game in the league cup. It was the year 1973 and there were nearly 44,000 supporters at the ground that night.

I can remember a couple of my school friends and I standing on Manchester Road which was a long road next to the football ground. I stood and watched hundreds of lads fighting each other with sticks and bottles and the police chasing them with batons and police horses.

At the time it seemed exciting and it would set me on a roller-coaster ride over the years as I followed the Bolton Wanderers.

The latter years at school were quite enjoyable. The teachers weren't as strict. We even had our own common-room where we were allowed to smoke. On the odd occasions we used to go into a pub called The Grapes for a few beers at dinner time. As a result I was sometimes sent home for being drunk and suffered my father's anger and brutality.

All this would come to an end when I was sixteen and my father came home drunk. He hit me for no reason and it was then that I retaliated and stood up to him.

Whether through fear are revenge, I gave him a good beating for all the abuse and brutality he had done to me and my mother over the years. After that he never raised a hand to me or my mother again.

I had suffered from his brutality for years. I never knew why he treated me like that but I blame him for all the wrongdoing I did later in my life. All I ever wanted was to be loved and accepted and I think that was why I got involved in the school fights, the gangs and the troubles at football matches. My friends gave me more respect and love than my father ever gave me. They were more of a family to me than my father ever was.

Getting up for school was hard work for me at the best of times and my dad used to shake me until I was awake.

I was fourteen at the time and I remember one morning I was getting ready for school when my dad shouted upstairs to come down. It always took me about forty minutes to wake up and get myself ready for school. I was always half-asleep eating my breakfast which usually consisted of cornflakes and toast which I used to eat on my way to school. Anyway my father was waiting for me in the front room and it was there that he dropped a bombshell.

He said, "Sit you down lad. I have something to tell you." He then told me that he had spoken with Mr Flannigan who owned the local paper shop and he arranged for me to do a paper round in the mornings. I was gobsmacked.

I replied nervously, "I don't want to do it as I have to go to school."

He just bawled at me like he always did and I had to stand to attention and not move an inch while I listened to him. Otherwise I would have got a slap for my troubles. My father told me I would be helping out the family, "Money is hard to come by, lad," he then told me. "You will start at six in the morning and the paper round will take about an hour and half at the most."

Nothing surprised me any more with my father, he had me doing all kinds of things from stealing coal to pinching wood from the building sites, to keep the house warm and for us to have hot water.

I just bit my tongue and went to the paper shop to see Mr Flannigan the shop owner. He told me all the 'ins and outs' and what time I was to start in the mornings. At that time in the early seventies being a paper boy was a low standing job with relatively low pay and it meant me braving cold, dark and inhospitable weather. But nevertheless I had to do it, not just because my father told me but I was helping my mother so I just went along with it.

The first time I delivered papers, I was escorted around and shown the route and how to deliver papers through the letter box and so on. The second day I was given a card with the house numbers on so I knew which houses to deliver the newspapers to.

Paper distribution was a fairly simple job. I used to hate doing the Saturday and Sunday rounds because of the excess of magazines, which severely added to the overall weight. Also they were prone to slipping out of the papers before delivery. It was a pain so I used to throw the magazines in the bin to lighten my load.

I was paid ever Sunday night and I was very lucky if my dad gave me anything. In fact the only spending money I used to get was from my grandma who we all called, 'little nanny.' She used to live with us at the time and it was only sixpence but it was sufficient to hit the penny tray before I went to school. I did have my own scams. I used to nick all the free gifts out of the magazines and the comics and I also used to pinch bottles of milk from people's door steps and sell them to my school friends.

The paper round did have its pitfalls not just because of the cold and wet dark mornings but the number of times I was bitten by the house-holder's dogs putting newspapers through the letter box. I had been attacked by stray dogs and even chased off strangers for the fun it. Delivering newspapers was becoming more difficult for me as the days passed by so I used throw them in the bin and go to school. Getting up at six o'clock, at the crack of dawn and freezing my nuts off and getting wet through on occasions had taking its toll on me.

I didn't need to pack the job in. I was sacked as a result of the number of complaints from the customers ringing Mr Flannigan complaining about the free gifts missing from the magazines and comics, and not receiving their newspapers.

Mr Flannigan, to his credit, never told my dad the truth; he left it to me to tell him.

My dad wasn't happy. But I just told him it was too dangerous as I had been chased a few times by strangers and I was too scared.

I only did the paper round for about three months I wasn't happy to do it as I was forced to do it. But you know the saying that if you are forced to do something against your will, you will rebel. It was something that I would became very good at over the years. (cheers dad!)

I left school at the age of sixteen with no qualifications. I left on a Friday and I started work on the Monday morning. Looking back now, I wish I could change things. There is a saying, *if I knew then, what I know now; maybe things could have been different.*

Chapter nine

The Farnworth gangs

The troubles carried on. I was accepted into the gang-culture with local gangs in Farnworth and we would test ourselves against our arch enemies the Little Hultoners.

I was brought up in a house of full of violence; looking at the clock and living in fear of my father coming home drunk and giving me a good beating. The rules were so strict. I wasn't allowed to have fun like normal children and I was not allowed to bring girls home. It was, therefore, a natural thing to rebel against my father wishes. I just wanted to be free and live a normal life. For me this involved joining a gang and being accepted. To me, at the time, this just looked normal. Even though being in a gang involved occasional violence, I didn't realise at the time that I was jumping out of the frying pan and into the fire.

I was just an immature kid who was rebelling against his father. I was getting rid of my anger and frustration on other people. This was one way of coping with it.

I was 15 years old and I was already battle hardened and scared with the beatings I had received from my father and the shenanigans I got up to at school.

I had already had dealings with the police on a regular basis and crossing paths with the 'infamous Sergeant Swann' was a regular pastime for me. I just looked at all this as if I was a loveable rogue who just liked a bit of fun and a laugh; a bit of adventure and an excuse to keep away from my father's wrath. It all was all tied up with gang culture. We used to all meet up at the row of shops we called Highfield which was just at the top of the road where my house was situated.

All my friends would gather there most nights. There were a good thirty of us and we were always smoking and drinking. We decided to call ourselves the Highfield Boot Boys.

We would test our strength against other gangs in Farnworth. They were from other estates and called themselves names like the Greenlanders and the Farnworth Central Boys but our ultimate test would always be against the Little Hultoners.

Little Hulton was built as a overspill estate in Salford near Manchester and the little Hultoners or 'Spillymies,' as we called them, were mainly Manchester United supporters whereas most of us from Farnworth were Bolton Wanderers supporters.

There was always hatred between our local rivals as my father, being a Bolton Wanderers supporter, always spoke of the rivalry between his team and Manchester United.

I remember being chased by a skinhead with a carving knife. He was wearing a black Crombie and white 'skinners' which was the fashion at that time. Luckily for me, he couldn't catch me as I could run faster than him.

Fighting on the Bridge would become a regular occurrence most nights and even spilled over into both our territories. As my face became better known to the Spillymies they would wait for me by the bus stop when I came home from school and even outside my house.

I even got dragged off a bus once and had a serious good hiding from some Little Hultoners. I still have a few scars to this day, to prove it. Living in Farnworth at that time was a dangerous pastime, but it was all fun and games. Getting a bit of a kicking was part and parcel of being in the gang. In any case, I was used to being black and blue so it was no novelty to me.

Whenever Manchester United played away we were always on the bridge lying in wait and we bricked many a coach carrying Manchester United fans, such was the hatred we had for them.

In 1974, I had just turned sixteen at the time; Bolton played Manchester United at home at Burnden Park on a Saturday. We already knew that the Little Hultoners would cross the bridge in large numbers. So we planned for weeks that we would wait for them there. It was our idea to embarrass them before they entered our territory and try to take over Farnworth.

We all met up bright and early on the bridge. There must have been a good hundred and fifty of us from all the estates in Farnworth. We made our way to the top of the fly-over bridge which separated Farnworth from little Hulton and we just waited there to see if they would turn up. It wasn't long before they came and they were in large numbers. There were hundreds of them. Many of them were skinheads and were wearing black Crombies which were a fashion they liked at the time. They also had white skinners on and most of them were a lot older than me. Nearly all of them had red and white silk scarves round their necks and most were wearing black boots which seemed to go half way up their legs.

I have to admit I was 'shitting' myself and as I started to disappear to the back there was an almighty roar and the battle began.

There were people lying on the floor covered in blood. Bricks and bottles were flying over our heads. There were fights all over the bridge with plenty of one-to-one battles going on. I was hit a few times but I stood my ground. It wasn't long before the police sirens could be heard and it was now every man for himself. Police chased us with dogs through the long grass in a farm field.

I escaped with a few others but some weren't so lucky and were heavily punished in the magistrate's courts at a later date.

The fighting continued for months after that until the police got on top of it. As for the event on the bridge, the Farnworth lads did themselves proud. They held the bridge and embarrassed the Manchester United fans. It was a different story at Burnden Park where the red army, as the Manchester United fans were known at that time, then ran amok and took over Bolton.

There is still a bitter rivalry to this day with Little Hulton but not on the scale it was in those days.

I received a few beatings but it was all part and parcel of being part of a gang and at that time it was just the norm.

It wasn't so long after that when I left my family and home town and moved on to pastures new and the violence didn't stop there. I moved onto a bigger stage; it was called 'football violence.' It was a roller- coaster ride following my beloved Bolton Wanderers all over the country fuelled by drink and troubles.

Chapter ten

The day the abuse came to an end

Since the age of four I had suffered at the hands of my father, he never told me his reasons and he never said he was sorry.

I always thought he was a coward and a bully, not just with me but with my mother who also suffered from his brutality over the years.

I was brought up in a house full of violence and fears; checking the clock when my father was coming home from the pub, worrying most days about what kind of mood he would be in. I blame my father for sending me down the wrong path.

I got involved in petty crime and football violence and running with the Farnworth gangs. I didn't know any different. I thought they were just the normal things young lads did at that time.

I lost count the number of times I was punched in the face and suffered black eyes and nose bleeds.

I can never forget the number of times I cried on my school desk, too afraid to say anything to anybody in case I got another beating.

Nowadays there would have been an investigation and I would have had proper protection. As for my father he would have been behind bars for a very long time.

However, I can remember some good times when there was no abuse but that was because my father was in prison but I didn't find this out until later in my life.

His actions towards me made me more rebellious and made it easier for me to hang around with the wrong crowd and get involved in crime and violence.

I lost count of the number of times I tried to run away from home, but at the age of fourteen, as you will already have read, I ran away to Paris.

I remember crying on the top deck of the ferry boat sailing to Calais in France because I was missing my mother but I was too afraid to go back home.

I also remember, on the day of my grandma's funeral when I was fifteen, my father punched me in the face for no reason. Whenever he was drunk or upset I was on the receiving end of his fists.

But one day all this abuse came to a sudden end.

I was sixteen years old, had just left school and started work at William Walker's, a tannery in Bolton which processed leather. By this time I was already hardened from being involved in gangs and football violence. I could handle myself a lot better and I wasn't a coward any longer, or so I thought.

On the day the abuse came to an end I set off to work as normal in the early morning, saying goodbye to my father who was fine at that time of day.

I came home as usual at half past four and got changed. Then I had my tea. My father was out, as normal, in the Flying Shuttle, a pub just at the top of our street. I was just watching the television when I heard the front door open. It was my father. He staggered into the front room, drunk as usual. He headed straight for the telly and turned it to a different channel. All I said to him was, "I was watching that."

He tried to punch me. It was then that I retaliated through fear or anger, I don't know which. I jumped up and I started to throw punches all over his body. I grabbed his head and put it in a headlock and carried on punching him in face.

It wasn't long before he was yelping out in pain and crying like a baby. I then threw him on the floor and kicked him. I shouted at him. "That's for all the abuse you did to me and my mother over the years and now it is payback time."

I looked at my mother and she smiled. She then put five pounds into my hand and I went out. I stayed out until the early hours so I could calm down and also; I was hoping that when I did go home he would be in bed.

It was 2.00 am when I arrived back home and I sneaked round to the back of the house so I could look through the back window praying that my mother was still up.

But to my horror I saw my dad's face through the window. I have to admit I was very worried, as I didn't know what kind of reaction I would get from him. I walked to the back door and he was there waiting for me. His face was a mess. He had a black eye and his cheeks were badly swollen. He told me to get in quickly before he gave me a slap. I walked through the door expecting a hiding but it never came.

I went straight to bed and in the morning my mum said to me, "I always knew you would get your revenge one day."

I wasn't proud of what I did to my father. I just wished it could have been different. All I ever wanted was for him to love me.

After that day he never touched me or my mother in anger again.

It wasn't long after that event when I left home but I always went back. I missed my mother. She was always there for me and was always a shoulder to cry on. She was my rock and she would prove that many times in the coming years.

My mother and father did separate a few years later and she met a wonderful person called Jack They eventually got married and had a wonderful thirty odd years together until he recently died of cancer.

He was the father that I never had and I truly loved him. God bless jack. I will always miss and love him.

Why didn't you say you're sorry?
I felt your wrath your hand
The pain, the tears
I cried a thousand tears

Why didn't you say you're sorry?
The house full of violence and fears
I cried a thousand tears

I cried on my school desk
All alone and in pain I lived in fear
The clock tick-tock
The door opened
He was here

I felt your wrath, your hand
Blood, marks and tears
Shaking with fear
The nightmare was here

I ran away across land and sea
All alone and in fear

I returned to a house full of violence and fears
I cried a thousand tears

All I wanted was your love
Why didn't you say you're sorry?

Chapter eleven

William Walker's

I had finished school in April 1974 and my last day at school was a happy one. We didn't do any work; we just had a laugh with the teachers.

A few of my friends went to the Grapes pub which was just facing my school in Dixon Green, Farnworth. One of my friends went to the bar to order drinks as most of us only looked about fourteen years old. Jimmy, however, who went to the bar, looked easily about twenty. He already had a 'tash and a beard. We used to call him 'animal' as he had more hair than a werewolf.

We had a few drinks of bitter and a good laugh. I was quite drunk and falling all over the place as I could get drunk on just two pints.

The landlord eventually kicked us out and told me, with a bit of sarcasm, that it was past my bedtime and my mother would be missing me. I said goodbye to my school friends and I staggered to my house. Along the way, I bought a few packets of polo-mints so my dad couldn't smell alcohol on my breadth.

When I arrived home I remember my mum opening the door. I fell over and collapsed on the floor to the amusement of my mother.

After a few hours sleep I sobered up and went downstairs. There, my father dropped a bombshell. He said, "Sit you down, lad. Now then; you start work at the tannery on Monday at 7.30 in the morning. I got you a job," he explained. I looked at him in sheer shock. "A job?" I stuttered.

My father replied, "Yes and good money too." I was gutted I had just left school and I wanted to have a few weeks break with all my friends and have some fun.

The weekend passed much too quickly for me. It was over before it had hardly started. Monday morning arrived. I was very apprehensive as I was unsure what to expect. Needless to say, I didn't sleep much the night before.

Walkers Tannery was founded 1823 by William Walker formerly of Houghton-Leskerne, Co. Durham. The original tannery was in King Street. Operations were transferred to Ridgway Gates in 1828. Tanning began at Rose Hill in 1850. The Railway Tannery, also at Rose Hill, opened in 1895. The firm also owned Bark Street Tannery, which it took over in 1864. The former Jackson's corn mill in Weston Street, Great Lever, was purchased for the manufacture of "Dri-Ped" leather in 1919. Subsidiary companies included Dri-Ped Ltd and Bolton Leathers Ltd. The origins of the Walker Property Co. Ltd lie in the purchase of land in Manchester, in 1876, upon which the Grosvenor Hotel was built.

I reported to work bright and early I arrived in plenty of time to have a nosey to get a feel of the place.

My first impression was the smell. The stench was overpowering to the point I felt nauseous.

The department in question, where I was to work, was called the lime-yard. It was where they used to put the animal hides in lime pits.

I couldn't believe my dad had got me the job there, I muttered to myself, as I reported to the office and introduced myself.

Mr Scholes, who was the foreman at that time, said, "Come on lad, follow me."

He showed me where to clock in and out and then pointed out to me where the changing rooms were.

He provided me with some blue overalls which were way too big and handed me some black boots which were also a size too big for me. The foreman then said sarcastically, "Hurry up then lad; get a move on." I was then shown round some of the departments where I would be learning my trade. All the time the Foreman was waffling down my ear trying to explain that tanning is the process of treating skins of animals to produce leather. He just reminded me of an old school teacher; he meant well but talked too much.

I started my training in a department called 'curriers.' I worked on a machine where they used to press the leather. I found it boring and very slow.

I was introduced to some members of the staff who were all a lot older than me. Mary, who was in her fifties, was very sweet and always looked after me; Andy Larkin who I called 'the midget' because he was so small and Eric Yates who used to talk like Kenneth Williams out of the Carry on Films. They were all characters in their own way.

Practical jokes started the following day. The midget (Andy Larkin) told me to go to the office and ask the foreman for a long stand. Like a good lad I went off and knocked on the office door and went in. The foreman said, "Come in lad, what can I do for you?"

"Andy sent me for a long stand."

The foreman smiled and said, "Wait over there lad." After what seemed like half an hour but was no more than a few minutes he spun round with a big grin on his face. He then said, "Do you think you have stood there long enough now lad?" As the words sunk in I soon realised that they were joking with me.

The foreman was laughing his socks off as I muttered under my breath, "For fuck sake."

Quick as a flash he replied, "Watch your language lad."
I walked back embarrassed as hell.

They were all laughing at my expense. I felt such a jerk. I didn't know whether to laugh or cry.

The practical jokes carried on for a while. Another example; I was told I would need a left-handed screwdriver. But the classic one was when I was working on the spraying machines adding colour to the leather. I was told to go for some tartan paint, only to realise half way there that they were pulling my leg. One particular payday to my horror, I misplaced my wage packet. If I looked in my locker a dozen times, I looked again and again. All afternoon I was worried about facing my father and telling him that I had lost my wage packet. The first bell went to say work had ended and it was time to get ready to clock off. My legs were shaking as I was worried about facing my dad as he had already told me, "No money, no bed."

I was nearly in tears leaving the factory, when the midget (Andy) shouted me over and said. "Have you lost something lad?"

I replied, "My money." He held his hand out and gave me my pay packet. I cried and cuddled him, I was so relieved.

From that point on I put my wage packet in my locker along with my all clothes.

The money I was earning every week meant I could afford to go and watch my beloved Bolton Wanderers home and away, up and down the country, every week. Even after paying my dad for my board and lodgings I was still left with plenty money to do what I pleased.

After a while I found out that my dad was spending the money I gave him on himself, - drinking and gambling. So I started to give a bit of money to my mother to help her out without my dad's knowledge.

The months went quickly by and my bank account got bigger. I could afford most things in life. The money also got me into trouble as I could afford to go out drinking in certain bars. I started meeting more girls and that led to conflicts with their boyfriends; and I was still getting into trouble with the police because of alcohol related trouble.

My working career at William Walkers Tannery would soon come to an end. I decided to move away from home to a bed and breakfast in Swinton. I wanted to get away from home for various reasons.

After a chance meeting in a pub with a stranger I would end up on a journey which would turn my who life upside down and involve another journey to Paris and a living nightmare in the French foreign legion.

Chapter twelve

A place called Bolton

Bolton has always had a good and proud history. It is well known for being an industrial town and for its old terraced houses and cobbled streets. It is also famous for its smoking chimneys, old men wearing flat caps and clogs and smoking the old pipes. I used to listen to all the tales about the old times with excitement every time I visited my grandparents. They were always good at spinning yarns. My granddad used to say in his broad Bolton accent. "Sit thee down lad, I'll tell thee a few stories."

I used to love the old war stories. His best one, I remember him telling me, was when he was having his supper and the sirens went off. The rest of the family fled into the outhouse in the back garden.

He told me that he muttered, "I'm staying put. I'm not wasting my food on a Krout. (a nick name for a German.) If my time is up, I'll die with a full belly."

He always made me chuckle he was a real character. He was mad on football, a Bolton Wanderers fanatic and I listened with enthusiasm about the times he went to Burnden Park, the home of Bolton Wanderers. Nat Lofthouse was his idol and he told me many a tale about him and when he had the pleasure of meeting him. The famous footballer became a regular visitor to my grandparent's house and that was something my mum is still proud of. He disliked Manchester United and I think the rivalry has carried on through the generations of my family.

I found it difficult getting served in the bars in the town centre in my early teens. I always got served in a bar called the Nags Head. It was full of under-age drinkers but nevertheless it was a good night out; a place where you could get drunk and have a good dance.

Bolton had its dark side too. At the weekends all the bars where full and Bradshawgate and Deansgate were full of drunken revellers; fist fights or brawls were common. Many a time on Bradshawgate, glasses and bottles were being thrown on either side of the road. If you wanted to get the leg over, you headed for the Bus Inn. This was a local night-club well known for 'slags' or 'old birds.' You were always guaranteed a knee trembler there.

I remember going to the Palais; it was a local night-club where everybody used to go after the last orders in pubs. I always made sure I had had enough drink before I went in as the drinks were so expensive. However, it was great for dancing and picking up the local tottie. It was here I learned my trade as sex was always on the menu.

There was also Scamps, another night-club on Bradshawgate. It was a rough place with fighting on the dance floor and the battles with the bouncers were guaranteed every Saturday night.

Yates Wine Lodge was always a favourite of mine in the 1970s. It was always packed to the rafters. It was nothing special but I remember seeing sawdust on the floor and the large queues at the bar waiting to be served. Behind the bar there were lots of barrels filled with Australian wines. It was famous for its 'docs' a small Australian wine which I used to drink before I went on the local beer. You had the usual local idiots who visited the place and drunken fights were quite common, most nights. I remember on one occasion the entrance doors came crashing open when a bloke came running in covered in blood and just behind I saw a police horse following him with the copper bending down so not to catch his head on the door entrance.

Ye Olde Man & Scythe was another favourite of mine over the years. This pub dates back to 1251. People had been drinking there for more than 750 years! It's the third oldest pub in England and one of the oldest in the entire world. The building has gone through some renovations since its inception, but many of the original parts still remain. The chair in the display case was occupied by James Stanley, the 7th Earl of Derby, on October the 15th, 1651 as he ate his last meal there. He was then taken outside and executed for his support of Charles Stuart and the Royalists during the English Civil War. It also well known for its ghost which vacated the place but more so for its cider which I got drunk on, on many occasions. The pub ceiling was low and if you didn't lower your head you would suffer with a cracked head. I enjoyed many a night in the Ye Olde Man and Scythe and still patronise the place to this day.

Bolton in the 70s and 80s was always very lively and attracted people from as far away as Liverpool. There was always coach parties from various towns and this didn't always go down very well with the locals. As a result sadly, stabbings were the norm in those days.

The weekends were becoming like the Wild West and Bolton was one of the first towns in the country to receive video cameras to try to stop all the trouble.

I had some great times drinking in Bolton and I suffered a few drunken nights in the police cells for my troubles but it was all a learning curve for me. Pulling girls with my mates at the weekends was something I always looked forward to and I lost count of the number of times I took a girl home or had a knee trembler on the way but it was all good fun at the time. As for the fighting, yes I did get involved in a few but that was the way it was in those days. The 70s and 80s were magical times for me in Bolton for many reasons and some of the memories I will always cherish.

Chapter thirteen

Nevada rink

The Nevada Roller Rink on Spa Road, Bolton was another of those great Bolton institutions that served us so well. Hundreds of skaters would head to the roller rink several nights a week from all over the North West. It was an amazing place to socialise, skate, dance and generally meet the opposite sex.

It was, in its heyday in the 1960's and 1970's and I first started to go to the Nav as the locals preferred to call it in 1974. I was sixteen and earning a good wage at the time so regular visits to the Nav weren't a problem. I remember my first time vividly, after collecting my roller skates I was showing off trying to impress the girls, like you do, when I slipped down the four or five steps to the area that sold soft drinks. I fell on top of two girls who were not very amused. I sprained my ankle and had to stand and watch for the rest of the evening! Oh the embarrassment. The following day I suffered with the aches and pains at work and at the end of the shift my ankle had swollen so much that they had to cut my boot off. My foreman Mr Scholes sarcastically said it will cost you for a new pair of boots. I laughed and said I only need a left one.

It would be another week before I went back to the Nav and even then my ankle was still sore. It was a Saturday night and a dance night. I could never get passed the bouncers on the upper floor where the alcohol was served as they were very keen. I never had any problems getting served in most pubs in and around town but the bouncers there did an excellent job stopping underage drinkers, much to my annoyance. So trying to impress the girls with a coke in your hand didn't always cut it. There was an event called the 'Spotlight,' if I remember correctly, where the girls had to wait to be chosen to skate in the dance. The first time I did a spotlight dance was with a girl from Wigan. She was called Angela and she was very sexy for a pie-eater (that's what Wiganer's were called.) I thought I had won the pools. I could see by the looks on my mates faces that they approved and getting envious looks made me feel ten feet tall. After a few dances with her she asked me if I was going to buy her a drink. I took her straight to the soft drinks bar and asked her what she wanted to drink? She replied that she wanted to go upstairs, meaning she wanted an alcoholic drink.

I called her bluff knowing that I had already been refused entrance early in the night. She backed down but I replied not to worry as I had a small bottle of vodka in my pocket and we could share it with some coke. By end of the night we both finished the bottle off and our embraces became more passionate towards the end of the evening. I don't know if it was the testosterone or the vodka but I went straight for her breasts as I couldn't take my eyes off them with her wearing a low cut top. I put my hand under her white top and slid my hand on to her breast. It must have been there for a good five seconds before I got a good slap across my face and told in no uncertain terms this was not the place. She stood up and I thought I had blown it as she started to walk off and then she stopped and said, "Are you coming are what?" I stood up, unsure what was coming next. She went to collect her coat and we left the building.

She held my hand and took me down Chorley Street. We then turned right underneath the road bridge. She then turned round to face me and said this was the place. We started to kiss and then she unzipped my pants and slid her hands on to my crotch and started to caress me. In the mean time I had unclipped her bra and started to caress her ample breasts.

I was tingling all over my body and before I knew it we were having sex standing up against the wall. It was almost over before it started as I was too excited. Before we could speak we heard voices so we both got dressed quickly. I started to move but she pulled me back and we continued kissing and she said we still had time for more before her mum picked her up.

When the people had passed she put my hand on her crotch and told me to stroke her gently. She unzipped my pants and slid her hand in. I wasn't aroused even though I was feeling it.

She said don't worry I will help you with that. She knelt down and pleasured me and it soon achieved the desired effect.

Whilst waiting for her mum I couldn't resist asking where she had learned all that. (I knew she was a similar age to me.) She just replied with a large smile.

A car pulled up and it was her mother. She smiled and then said, "See you next week."

I met up with my mates and they asked me where I had been? I just smiled and said I'll tell you another time.

The Nav was becoming a weekly visit now and at the weekends they used to have bands playing and disco nights.

I lost count the number women I chatted up but I wasn't always successful. 'Some you win and some you lose,' but it wasn't from the lack of trying.

Lads from all over the North West came to the Nav so football rivalries extended to the dance floor as well as the football grounds. We had scuffles with lads from Blackburn and Wigan and Preston. But our main rivals were Manchester United and there were many scuffles with them.

On one such occasion some of my mates and I had an altercation with some Manchester United fans on the dance floor which continued outside. It was four against four and we completely annihilated them. It wasn't long before they were on their toes, (meaning they ran away.)

We thought it was all over so Ste Cooke and I made our way to the Albion pub as there was a coach picking up the Bolton fans at 12 am and then travelling down overnight for the game in Plymouth. It was only 11.30 pm so we were the first to arrive and we unfolded our large BWFC flag.

In the distance we could see a large group of people heading towards us so we started to sing, "Come on you whites," thinking they were more Bolton fans coming for the coach.

They responded, "Come on you Reds," as they charged towards us. We recognised some of the lads. It was the same of lads from the fight earlier but with all their mates. I just said to Ste, "Run," and we split. I was chased right across the bus station.

I found myself fighting with two of the faster ones who had caught up with me and I was holding my own until more arrived. Then, I was kicked to the floor and I was only saved by a bus driving towards us forcing them to stop. Luckily for me the bus doors opened and I jumped on and the driver drove off with the sound of fist and feet pounding on the side of the bus as we drove away.

When we were clear, he dropped me off and told to get home lad. But me being me, I made my way back to Albion. By this time there was a coach full of Bolton supporters minus Ste Cooke who was nowhere to be seen. Even though I was black and blue I was more upset about losing my Bolton flag.

I went for a few more years to the Nav watching live bands and skating. It will always stand out as some of my happier times.

It was a sad day when the people of Bolton lost the great institution known as the Nav (the Nevada) as it was burned down in 80s.

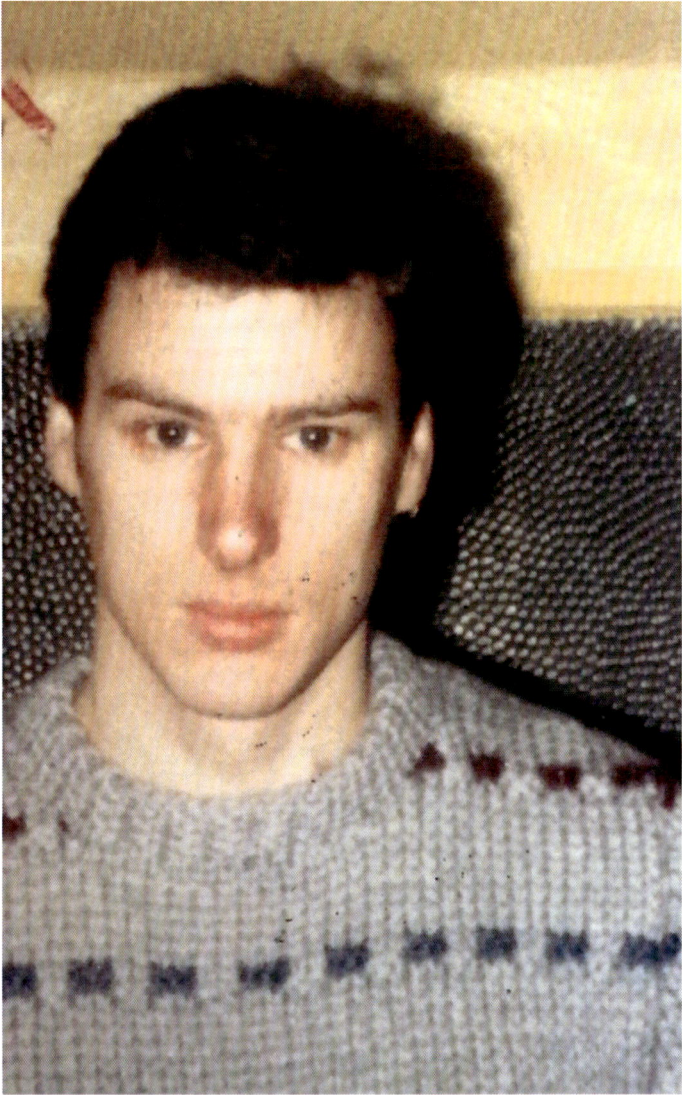

The author at eighteen

Chapter fourteen

The French Foreign Legion

At the age of eighteen I decided to leave home once again and this time I was more determined to leave for good. Even though the abuse had stopped with my father the pain and the anger I felt towards him had never left me. I had made my mind up that I had to cut loose from my mother's apron strings; it was time to find my own way in the world. My mother always knew that I would leave one day to seek for my own way in life.

The day had arrived, my suitcase was packed. I knew where I was staying as I had already done my homework. I wanted to live outside Bolton away from my family and friends.

I wanted to start afresh in a new place and to make new friends. I hugged my mother and told her how much I loved her. As usual she stayed calm and tried not to show her feelings.

Before I left she held my hand and then put something in my pocket. Then she said to me, "Ian keep out of trouble and look after yourself."

I just smiled and then I left. I never said goodbye to my father as he kept well out of my way. My dad showed no compassion or any interest and our feelings towards each other were mutual. As I was walking up the path I put my hand in my pocket and felt some paper. I looked and it was thirty pounds in an elastic band. I looked up and my mother was smiling and waving at me through the window.

I waved and smiled back and then I turned away and carried on walking. I never turned back as I was frightened I would change my mind and go back home.

I made my way to the bus stop at the top of my road and while I was waiting, I was reminiscing about my younger days, the troubles I used to get up to. I could see the police houses where Sergeant Swann used to live and the shops where I used to hang around with my friends. It was here that I had had to grow up very quickly and learn how to defend myself. The petty thieving, the gang fights and the run-ins with the infamous Sergeant Swann; it was now time to put it all behind me and move on to pastures new.

The bus arrived and I jumped on and sat down. I looked through the window as the bus was leaving. I had a big smile on my face. I thought to myself I had some great memories but my troubles were over. It was a new beginning now or so I thought.

I stayed in a bed-and-breakfast in Swinton. It was cheap and just a few miles from Farnworth and it was easy access to get to and from work.

Swinton is a town within the City of Salford, in Greater Manchester. (Historically in Lancashire)

I arrived in the afternoon at the B & B and I was met by the owner at the door. He introduced himself and took me to my room.

The room was not big; in fact it was quite small with a bed and a small bed-side cabinet. There was a wardrobe and that was it. The carpets were brown and worn and the curtains were a dirty cream colour and they weren't hanging correctly as the curtain rail was hanging off the wall.

The owner then showed me the bathroom which had to be shared with the other guests. It was smaller than my old box-room at home.

It was certainly a wake-up call and reality started to sink in. I soon realised that there was no place like home.

I unpacked what clothes I had and I decided to have a few hours nap. I found it difficult to sleep, however, as my thoughts kept drifting back to my youth and my bond with my mother.

I was soon settled and the trips to work every day took my mind off other things. One night I was sitting alone in a pub near to where I was staying. Little did I expect a chance encounter with a stranger that would lead me to another journey and one that would leave me scared for the rest of my life?

It all started with, "Hi mate, do you mind if I join you?" He introduced himself and said his name was Paul Smith. The conversation soon got on to football which was a favourite passion in life for us both. He was a Manchester United supporter and with me being a Bolton Wanderers supporter it didn't go down too well with me. However, with me being alone, I carried on with the conversation.

Paul smith was nothing special to look at. He was tall and skinny with long scruffy brown hair.

He stuttered quite badly which seemed to improve the more he drank and throughout the evening I got to learn his life-story.

He had been in and out of Borstal (A Borstal was the term used to describe a system of juvenile detention centres that existed in the United Kingdom for most of the 20th century) and in and out of adult prisons.

The conversation soon got round to the French foreign Legion as he started to open up about his life of crime.

He then told me he was on the run from the police and if they caught him, he was going to get sent down again.

That's when he turned round and told me he wanted to join the French legion in a bid to be a better person, as they give you a new identity; a new name, passport and a new life and a new family. The French Foreign Legion would look after you with a pension and a new life.

I laughed out loud and told him he had watched too many films. I watched Beau Geste and I didn't fancy having my head stuck in the sand, to which he replied with a smile, "It's not like that Ian, I have looked into it."

That's when I realised he was serious and I started to wonder, would it erase my past of beatings at the hands of my father?

Paul then came straight out with it. "Why don't you come too?" Suddenly, it just seemed exciting, a new adventure.

I said "Yes" and we arranged to meet the following day. That's when I found out he had nowhere to stay. He had told me he was on the run from the police so I decided to smuggle Paul into the B & B.

We both talked quietly through the night. We were like two excited kids.

I asked Paul what age you had to be to join the legion.

He then replied, "18."

I then asked, "Where do you join-up for the legion?"

Paul responded "Paris".

I didn't know whether to laugh or cry and told Paul I ran away to Paris when I was fourteen.

We both just laughed and Paul said, "This time it will be better."

In the morning I went down for a full English breakfast (egg, bacon, tomatoes, fried bread with toast and a mug of coffee.) I smuggled a few bacon sandwiches out for Paul.

I packed a few essentials for my journey whereas Paul just had the clothes he was wearing along with his passport and about forty pounds which was from a cheque he had stolen.

I telephoned my boss at the place where I worked and told him I was sick and I didn't know when I would be coming back. Then we made our way to the post office where I paid for a temporary short-term passport and then we were off.

We caught a train from Piccadilly train-station to London. The journey down was uneventful and we then caught a train to Dover.

We weren't hanging around for long before we were on the ferry to Calais. As the ship sailed away I could see the white cliffs of Dover and for a spit second it brought back the memories and feelings of my first trip to Paris

The trip was still uneventful and the conversation between us was short as we only talked about football. I wonder now if it could have been our misapprehension and fear of the unknown preventing us from talking about what lay ahead.

After a couple of hours we arrived at Calais and we made our way to the bottom deck and ready to disembark.

We both just followed the queues until we had our passports checked and then we made our way to the train station.

When we arrived at the train station there were thousands of tourists of different nationalities from different parts of Europe. It didn't take us long to find the ticket-office. We then booked our relevant tickets to continue our journey to Paris.

The journey took just under four hours and soon passed. Paul had suddenly regained his enthusiasm. The conversation was non-stop about the French Foreign Legion and he was so excited about the prospect of being a soldier in the famous army.

On the other hand, I was slightly nervous and wary of what I was getting myself into. Before we knew it we had arrived in Paris.

We made our way out of the train-station and headed for the centre of Paris. I was so excited. I kept telling Paul that Paris was the most interesting city in Europe and probably one of the most amazing cities worldwide. People from all over the world, travel to Paris. They come to discover and experience this fairy-tale city. Paris was the city of love, inspiration, art and fashion. The night-scene, the Eiffel tower, I continued until he abruptly ended my conversation and told me we are not here to be a tourist but to enlist in the French Foreign Legion.

He then told me we must ask someone how to get to the Fort de Nogent as time was getting on.

We approached a French policeman. They are known as Gendarmes. We asked him how to get to the Fort de Nogent? He smiled and said, "The foreign legion?" He then said, "Follow me," in good English. "I will show you the bus to get you there."

He showed us the bus-stop where we were to catch the bus and then he laughed and walked off to our amusement.

We didn't wait too long as buses were quite frequent. We jumped on the bus and said to the driver, "Fort de Nogent?" He just replied, "Three francs."

We both paid the amount and sat down. The journey wasn't long but it was a very interesting trip. Nevertheless, I showed Paul the Eifel Tower and some of the places where I begged and tried to pick pockets.

The journey was short and the bus stopped and the driver shouted, "Fort de Nogent," so we got off and in the distance we could see a large building with an imposing arch and gates.

I said to Paul, "We are here. Are you sure you don't want to change your mind?"

He smiled and said, "Come on Ian, we have a new life now, a new future."

We reached the Fort and there was a traffic circle with a huge sign indicating *Legion Etrangere* off to the side.

There was what appeared to be a tree-lined driveway next to the sign that led down between two apartment buildings. We both walked to the sign. We walked down the driveway and eventually the stone walls and gate of a very ancient looking fortress came into view. There was no doubt in my mind that this was the place as above the gate were the words *Legion Etrangere*. At this point, I got a tingling sensation down my neck. The most complicated part of our trip was now over.

We walked through the gates and we were approached by what we took to be a legionnaire dressed in a blue boiler suit. Paul spoke and said we wished to join the legion.

The legionnaire gestured to us to follow him. He took us to a reception area where were met by another legionnaire who was sitting behind a desk.

We were then taken separately into different rooms. It was there that we handed over our passports. The legionnaire then asked me various questions about my age and country of origin. He then enquired if we had any criminal records. Were we wanted by the police? It was then that I started to worry about Paul; if he would tell the truth or would he lie.

I filled all the paperwork in and he explained all about the legion, the length of service and the army pensions etc.

I was then told I would have to have a medical before I was accepted into the legion. Then he said that I should go into another room and to get undressed as I was having a medical there and then.

I didn't wait long until one of the army doctors came in. He asked a lot of questions about my health and then I was subject to a thorough examination.

I was then told to get dressed and wait. After a few minutes I was escorted to another room where Paul was already there with a few other recruits.

It was here that I was told that I had to fill in the relevant forms before I could be accepted into the legion.

We were only at the centre for a few days and when it came time for us to leave the Fort (when there were enough of us and we had been through our preliminary medical examinations) we showered and dressed in our civilian clothes. We were then placed on a bus and taken to a large train station in Paris (I think it was Gare de Lyon.)

We rode on an overnight train to Marseille that stopped many times along the way. We had our own seats, but had to share the car with tourists and local commuters.

We were accompanied by three legionnaires but they were dressed in civvies. We were told by one of the legionnaires, a corporal I think, that we needed permission to go to the toilet or the bathroom so that they knew where we were.

The train journey was bad because I couldn't get any sleep. You could hear people walking up and down the train and some of the passengers even brought their dogs and you could hear them barking now and again. The most annoying was the conductor he would turn the lights on checking the passengers tickets.

When we arrived in Marseille, the sun was already up. We exited the train and made our way to another platform where we boarded a double-decker local commuter train to Aubagne. When we arrived in Aubagne, a bus was waiting to take us to Quartier Vienot, the HQ of the Legion.

The first thing we did at Aubagne was to get our pictures taken. They resembled prisoner mug-shots. Afterwards, we were marched a short way to a small white building which would be our home until either going to basic training or being dismissed. We walked around to a side door to the basement where we met a Corporal who would be with us the whole time we were there. We then had to strip down (including our underwear) to be naked. They issued us underwear, shorts, a T-shirt, socks and a really crappy pair of flat-soled zero-support zero-cushioning tennis shoes. Our names were then called one by one and we went up to a counter with our bag, (filled with the clothes we had just gotten out of.) There a legionnaire took inventory of what we had. I had to sign the inventory and then grab the military backpack and run around to the other side of the counter and sit down and wait with guys who had gone before me. The Corporal explained the rules to us (in French) with accompanying gesturing for emphasis. He was the boss. He's the Legionnaire. We want to be like him. We don't talk. We do what he says. The only place where you can talk and do what you want is in the back of the building. There, he said, we could talk, smoke, snort our cocaine if we wanted. He strongly recommended, however, that we spend our time running and doing push-ups. He said that in basic training there will be many push-ups. We were later shown to our room where we were assigned our bunks.

We woke up at somewhere around 3:30 - 4:00 am every day and were supposed to go to sleep at around 9:00 pm (you usually could not go to sleep until a couple of hours after 9:00 because most people in your room would keep talking.) We took showers before going to bed, and it was the same deal as in Paris - not enough time and a whole lot of guys scrambling for a few showers. The guys who got to the showers first tended to take their sweet time and the guys stuck at the end would have to rush. We had to clean our room everyday and fold our sheets a certain way immediately after waking up, and make the bed a certain way immediately before going to bed. When not on a work detail or taking a test, we sat in a large 'garden' behind the building that was devoid of grass. There, people tended to group together by language/ethnic background and talk with each other. There were probably over a couple of hundred guys there all the time. People seemed to disappear everyday and new faces appeared to replace them. Some people exercised, but most just sat around smoking and talking.

I received my first hair cut and to my horror they shaved off all my hair. I felt so naked. I was then kitted out with my new army uniform. My best friend was my new beret to cover the modesty of my bald head.

When I saw Paul I just burst out laughing his head was shaven like mine but he looked like a matchstick as he was so thin.

Life was pretty boring in the legion at the beginning. There was a klaxon (air raid siren) mounted on the roof of the building at the rear. When it went off, all the CEVs in the 'garden' would take off running -- just like a stampede -- towards the front of the building where there was a large tarmac that served as a formation area. We would have to quickly get into a block formation and stand at attention (known as 'gardez-vous.') When in block formation we would be split up to handle work details, or take tests, or go eat a meal, or be yelled at for something, or made to do push-ups, sit-ups, roll-over, or other punitive exercises. Many times, we would get called to the formation, then have to walk around the building en masse and pick up 'debris' (cigarette butts, trash, sometimes rocks, leaves, etc...). Sometimes we would have to go, 'weed the canal' next to the building. Mainly, picking up debris and weeding the canal were just busy work for us. Work details included cleaning our barracks, doing kitchen duty in one of several kitchens: either the main kitchen, a satellite kitchen elsewhere in the base, at Malmousque -- the Legion resort, or at the Legion retirement home. There were also non-kitchen work details at these locations as well as 'debris' collection elsewhere in the base. I wound up doing kitchen duty in the main kitchen a lot, mainly because I happened to be around after a meal when the mess hall (salles de manger) Corporal was looking for people to do kitchen duty. I really didn't mind because I found that, generally, the Legionnaires that worked in the kitchens were really cool guys who were [usually] pretty laid back. A major problem that develops at Aubagne is dehydration. It is very hard to stay adequately hydrated because you always have to drink from a tap and access to the interior of the building is restricted (even to go to the toilet.)

Paul and I became quite friendly with two lads; a lad from Dublin who we called paddy and a lad from Holland who we called Dutch for obvious reasons.

We would spend many an hour chatting about our experiences in our own countries and the reasons why we joined the legion.

Paddy pre-warned me about some of the cliques in the legion and I was told in no uncertain terms to keep my nose clean and not to get involved with anybody else's squabbles. He had seen a few legionnaires get a good hiding and it was taboo to tell tales to any senior officers. It would be a death sentence to anybody who grassed anyone up.

I looked at Paul with a worried look but he just burst out laughing and said stop worrying, "We are all family in here."

What happened next would turn my career in the legion upside down and become a nightmare which would haunt me for the rest of my life. It all started when I walked into the shower room with Paul and I saw three males of Arab descent beating up a male who was known to be a Jew. I intervened by grabbing one of the Arabs who I threw against the shower wall. I then punched one of the other Arabs who let go of the Jewish lad. The Jewish male then grabbed his towel and ran out. The attention turned to me. I was pushed against the wall and I was being punched and kicked at will. It was over before it started as more legionnaires came in to the showers. Before the Arabs left I was warned in broken English that my life was in danger and to watch my back.

I went crazy at Paul and I shouted why didn't he help me? His pitiful reply was that I was told to keep my nose clean and not to get involved. I grabbed Paul by the neck and called him a fucking coward and as I walked away he shouted to me not go to the officers and tell them what happened, as it would be a death sentence for me and it would not be safe for me to stay in the legion. I just looked at him in disgust. I got dressed and walked away.

I was only in the legion a couple of weeks and I was already regretting every minute.

I was still having medicals and doing physical tests and interviews and this carried on for days. I was doing plenty of running and sit-ups under the watchful eyes of the trainers. I heard if you failed the test you would be kicked out the same day.

I still had a few friends in the legion. Paddy and Dutch were always by my side and as for Paul he went into a shell. He wasn't the same person any more. He tried to avoid me when he could and we only ever spoke a few words.

Things turned from bad to worse in the early hours of the morning when I was asleep. I felt a hand running up and down my body. It woke me up. Besides my bed were two of the Arabs who attacked me in the shower. One of them put his hands over my mouth while the other one was trying to hold me down on the bed and tried to grab my penis.

I was kicking out like crazy. I was biting the Arab's hand as hard as I could.

Dutch jumped out of his bunk and ran to my aid.

The two Arabs ran off to their bunks. I was shaking with fear. My emotions were all over the place. I was disgusted I wanted to go to the shower and wash myself clean but I was too afraid to go in case they followed me in there.

Dutch sat on my bed for a few hours trying to calm me down. He kept telling I must not report it as things would look bad for me.

I didn't sleep all night and I was more determined now to watch my back and keep out of trouble.

I always made sure I was with Dutch and Paddy whenever I went for a shower and that I was never on my own.

My moods and my desire to be in the legion had changed. I had only been in the legion a few weeks but it was becoming a life sentence of fear and intimidation.

I was still getting the occasional punch and kick on the legs from the Arabs whenever it suited them to do so.

I couldn't retaliate as I would have been in serious trouble. I couldn't do a runner as I would have been charged with desertion.

Things came to ahead when I was having my breakfast and one of the Arabs threw a tray over me and spat in my face.

I wanted to kill him on the spot but Dutch held me down. The Arab walked away, laughing.

I told Dutch I was brought up with violence and been involved in gangs and football violence but this was on a different scale.

I have never been so afraid. I told Dutch I had only been in the legion a few weeks but I had to get out before I did something stupid.

Dutch replied, "Follow me. I will tell you how to get out of the legion."

I walked past the smirking Arabs and just smiled at them and gave them the 'wankers' sign. I passed Paul and he put his head down and ignored me. I shouted to him that he was also a 'wanker' and I walked out of the dining room.

Dutch and Paddy were waiting for me. I followed them into the toilets so we could speak in private.

I asked Dutch to tell me how could get out of the legion. He replied the only way was to harm myself. You will be kicked out of the legion for cowardice; a dishonourable discharge.

I shook both their hands and thanked them. I went to my locker and got hold off a razor blade. Then I cut a little on my wrist, enough to make it bleed. I let the blood run down my arm and on to my green uniform to make it look worse. Then I told Dutch to go and tell the Corporal. Within minutes the Corporal came running in. He slapped my face and called me a coward and told me to go and clean myself up then to report to his office straight away.

I looked at Dutch and Paddy and smiled and winked. Then I went to the toilet and cleaned myself up.

I knocked on the door of the Corporal's office and he shouted in his French accent, "Come in Mr Lomax." I went in and the Corporal was with an officer. I was then told to shut the door and sit down.

On the table were some documents. I was told I was being discharged from the legion and that I would not be allowed to return.

I signed my signature and then I was frog-marched into a small room. Inside I found my small suitcase containing the clothes I came in. I was told to sign another document for the items I received.

The corporal told me to strip off my uniform. While I was doing this he stood and watched.

He then kicked my army kit to one side and shouted to me to get dressed. He said the sooner I was off this camp the better.

I knew he was trying to humiliate me but I didn't care. I was going home. As soon as I was dressed he shouted, "Follow me, English coward."

I was taken to a counter where my passport was handed to me and a small packet with a few hundred francs which was my pay for the short time I was in the legion.

I signed some more documents then I was escorted off the camp in disgrace by two legionnaires. I was then put into an army jeep and taken to the train station. The jeep stopped, a door opened, I climbed out and without any words being spoken, they drove off.

My nightmare was over and so was my short career in the foreign legion. The train journey to Paris was a quiet one. I tried to erase the beatings and the attempted rape from my memories.

I can't remember much about the journey home but I never spoke about what happened in the foreign legion to anybody. I went home once again to my parents.

My mother was glad to see me and even my father had a smile on his face. My mother asked where I had been. I replied with a smile, "In the French Foreign Legion."

Chapter fifteen

Butlins

After the escapades in the foreign legion my father tried to get my old job back for me at William Walkers Tannery in Bolton but I had all ready burned my bridges with them and there was no going back. I really didn't care as I hated the job anyway and you had to understand at that time there was plenty of jobs available.

An opportunity soon appeared, working at Butlin's Holiday Camp in Somerset. I could not believe my luck. I have to admit I was hoping that it would be like a scene from the movies; all laughs, fun and plenty of girls.

So once more I was on my travels but saying good bye properly to my mother this time. It didn't seem as heartbreaking as I knew I would be coming back and I just looked on it as a long holiday.

Transport was provided from Bolton to Minehead and there were other pick-ups along the way. There was a party atmosphere on the coach and as more and more people joined the coach it became more exuberant.

The majority of people on the coach were teenagers. They came from all walks of life. At times it reminded me of coach trips going to away matches following my beloved Bolton Wanderers. The alcohol was passed around freely and quite a few of the passengers were getting intimate under the influence of drink.

We arrived at the camp only to be greeted by the security. My first thoughts were, *shit it's like joining the army*. We all collected our belongings and got off the coach, but a few of the passengers were turned away as they were too intoxicated; they weren't allowed on the camp.

We were then met by a member of staff who showed us our living quarters as it was late in the evening.

The first thing I noticed was that the sexes were segregated. I must admit I was hoping to share with a couple of girls who I had taken a shine to on the coach. And believe me, the security had dogs patrolling the girls quarters. The idea of being celibate was the last thing on my mind; to say I was deflated would be an understatement.

I was introduced to my new room-mate who was from Nottingham; he was built like a brick shit-house and cocky with it.

The following morning we all went for breakfast. It was a self-service with a great selection of food. After that we went for a short induction where we were allocated our jobs and provided with uniform which consisted of a blue jacket with a yellow collar and an ID badge.

The rules were then laid out. Being drunk on site, fighting or any sexual misconduct would not be tolerated. My first thoughts were that I had not come all this way to be a monk as rules are made to be broken.

The job I was allocated was working on the fair ground. The hours were great as they were only from nine till five, six days a week, with one day off. And that was great news for me as the evenings would be my own.

The first day at work I found out that I was helping out on the dodgems. The staff there showed me how to operate the controls, which were pretty basic.

This was when I was given my first bit of good advice. If I wished to impress any girls I fancied, I could let the ride go on longer than it should. That brought a huge smile to my face.

I just had to figure out how to smuggle girls past security. I was soon to find out the answer to that question as the following night I was awakened by noises which left me in no doubt that Nottingham had a girl in bed. I looked across the room and my jaw dropped. She was stunning and a holiday maker. I had to endure a sleepless night as Nottingham was giving her his all. In the morning I saw the full beauty of the girl. She was blonde with ample breasts. She gave me a knowing smile and she showed no embarrassment as I saw her naked flesh. It was hard for me to hide my growing excitement.

After she left I asked Nottingham how he sneaked her past security. He answered with his large cocky smile, "Just cross the security palm with silver."

As the days passed by I didn't need to chat up the girls. Believe me; I didn't need to chase them as I soon found out.

I got pally with a lad from Derby who was a total nutcase but great fun to be with. My first sexual encounter was with two girls who Derby had introduced to me. They weren't anything special but who was I to turn my nose up at the chance to get my leg over.

We sneaked passed the security guard and went straight into the girls chalet. Before I knew it my clothes were off. There was no foreplay; we got straight down to it. We said our goodbyes in the early hours and made our way back to our chalets.

The smile on my face was soon wiped off as Nottingham had tied my Bolton Wanderers scarf round a trunk on the top of a tree along with all my clothes.

Nottingham had locked me out of the chalet so I climbed the tree got my scarf and gathered my clothes and went to Derby's chalet. I was fucking furious; I wanted to kill him but Derby said, "You have to share a room with him so just let it lie. You will get back at him another time.

Two days later I found out that Derby had got back at Nottingham in the changing rooms by giving him a good hiding. Apparently, as I later found out, there was no love lost between Nottingham and Derby.

After that, I don't know what happened to Nottingham as I never saw him in my chalet or on the camp either but I didn't shed any tears.

The sexual encounters carried on and each week we would be rewarded with a new batch of eager girls. After three are four months of this I looked forward to a night off. Believe me, none of the girls wanted a lasting relationship, they just wanted a bit of fun like I did, with no strings attached.

One occasion that stood out from all the rest was when I was taken back to a girl's chalet only to find her sister was there. I was left in no doubt that I was there for both of them. Who was I to complain? I was completely fucked as each girl took me in turn several times. It was always a dream of mine to have sex with two girls; something which never happened again.

I did have some principles, as one night, a young women took me back to her chalet and we were both in a state of undress as soon as the door shut. As we made our way to the bed I noticed a small child in a single bed. I thought to myself this is wrong. I couldn't go through with it. I dressed quickly and told her I was sorry and left.

The months soon passed, sex became almost routine for me. Derby and I had booked a few days holiday so we could go and watch Bolton Wanderers play Wolves at Burnden Park in the last game of the season.

The night before we were due to go to the match, over a few beers at the bar it seemed a good idea that we should take a Union Jack flag and write on it BWFC. We already knew there was one problem; it was on a flag pole in the middle of Butlins grounds. After a few more beers I was to be found climbing the flag-pole because the ropes had got tangled. Derby who should have been keeping a look-out shouted, "Ian." When I looked down he was surrounded by security. I made my way down and we were frogmarched to the duty manager who told us get our bags and get off the site. By this time it was midnight. We collected the wages that were owed to us and we were escorted off the camp.

We slept rough that night in a bus-shelter and when it became light Derby and I made our way to the coach station. It was then that we said our final goodbyes and went our separate ways.

I arrived home and things hadn't changed; it was back to reality.

The next few years I was in and out of jobs. I even went back to Butlins in Phwelli. It was just as I remembered it. The girls were still on the menu but nicking flags was off limits. I did the full six months this time and kept a clean slate.

As for Derby I lost contact but I will never forget the friendship and the antics we both got up to.

Chapter sixteen

You're in the army now.

After all my escapades and troubles in foreign lands, I thought I had put a closure on that sort of thing but things were about to change.

One morning, while I was watching TV my mother and father came in to the front room. My father turned the TV off; my mother sat next to my father and he just came straight out with it

"Ian, you can't carry on in life with no purpose, getting into trouble with the police and being unemployed and just lazing about with your friends," he said.

"Tomorrow morning, your mother is taking you to the Army Recruitment Office in Great Moor Street Bolton."

"You're going in the army if you like it or not," my mother added. "It didn't do any of my brothers any harm and it will do you good and make you into a man."

I looked at my parents in complete horror and I shouted out, "You are joking aren't you?"

I never told my parents what happened to me in the French Foreign Legion and I thought to myself there's no way I'm going to go through all that again.

She just kept repeating, "Ian I'm serious. You are going into the army; it will change your life for the better."

She put her arms around me and said, "Please Ian, do it for me. I'm worried about the direction you are taking in life. I don't want you to end up in prison."

I will never know why I agreed. It could only be because I loved my mother and I knew she cared about me.

In the morning I got up and had breakfast. I was still hoping that she was joking but my smile was soon wiped off my face when she said. "Go and get dressed. We are going into Bolton to the Army Recruitment Centre."

I knew my mother was only doing what she thought was best me for me, so off we went. Even my sister Patricia came along.

I looked through the windows on the bus and I looked all around me and I muttered to myself that maybe it was a good thing to get away from Highfield and the troubles.

My mother held my arm and took me into the Army Recruitment Office and there in front of me was some kind of an officer in army uniform, sitting at his desk.

My mother told the officer this was her son and he wanted to join the army. If there would have been a hole in floor I would have dropped through it.

The officer told me sit down. He then asked me a few questions. "Have you been in trouble with the police?" to which my mother replied, "He's a good lad." This brought a huge smile to my face.

The officer told me, "There is much more to the army than military skill. You can go abroad. We will equip you with new skills, give you invaluable experience and develop strengths you didn't know you had."

He then asked me what qualifications I had. I replied that after I had left school I didn't take any exams. I went straight into a job.

Then the officer said you must take an entrance exam in English and Maths to see if we can accept you or not. This brought a huge smile to my face as I thought I was as thick as a barge pole and those were my two worst subjects.

I knew my chances of getting into army were slim so I was happy. My mother and sister then left as I had to do the test. The officer said, "You get thirty minutes per test, so take your time and good luck."

I made sure I would miss some of the questions out and answer a few of them wrong. I also made sure that I would finish the test-papers early.

The hour soon passed and the officer came back and took the test-papers from me. He said, "I won't be too long."

I was sure I was going to fail. The officer came back and said, "Congratulations you have passed." He shook my hand. I nearly collapsed with shock. I then signed some papers and I had just signed away three years off my life. My first thoughts were no more going to the football matches with my mates, no more women and my worst fears were remembering what happened in the French Foreign Legion.

The officer then told me I would be going to Sutton Coldfield Selection Centre for three days assessment and I would also learn where they would be sending me.

I left the recruitment centre disheartened. I met my mother and sister in a cafe in the town centre.

I walked through the door and my mum shouted over, "Have you passed?"

I simply said, "Yes." My mum and my sister were overjoyed and they both hugged me.

I sat down and my mother said, "I didn't think you'd pass the entrance exams."

I mumbled under my breath, "I wish I hadn't."

My sister Pat held my hand and said, "I'm so happy for you. What would you like to drink?"

I laughed and said I would have a large whiskey which put a smile on both their faces.

I knew deep down she meant well and was doing her best for me. I told them both I had to go Sutton Coldfield Recruitment Centre for three days and I would be assessed there as to which army base and regiment I would be sent to.

"I have a week of freedom before I have to go and I'm going to enjoy myself before I leave," I replied.

My mother told the whole street I was going in the army and she was so proud of me. Everywhere I went people were patting me on the shoulder, to my dismay.

The time had arrived. I was on my way to Sutton Coldfield in Birmingham on a coach with some other recruits. The journey didn't take long, just a few hours. We arrived at the centre but the coach was stopped at the barrier where some army personnel checked the driver's papers. I was scanning around as I sat there. It just reminded me of the time I spent at Fort de Nogent in the French Foreign Legion and that brought a lump to my throat. I was trying to calm my fears by saying to myself, *I'm in the British army and I will be well treated*. We all got off the coach carrying our suitcases and were taken into a large room.

A lance-corporal introduced himself to us and explained all what would be happening while we were there for the next three days.

We were then taken into quarters where we would be sleeping or bunking up as the army recruits called it. Then we all went for meal in the canteen. There was lamb sirloin and lots of other great choices on the menu.

For some reason I felt relaxed and the three years service went to the back of my mind.

I got pally with a few of the lads including Sean from Manchester and Dale from Blackburn.

Both were football fans and that was my favourite subject. I had good laughs with them and we spent a lot time together over the three days.

Sean supported Manchester United and I let him know how much contempt I had for them. And Dale supported Blackburn rovers who I disliked as well but it was all in good fun and we laughed about the rivalries between us.

During our stay there we had to do all kinds of physical tests, sit-ups and press–ups, general gym work and circuit work. We also did a written test and watched film shows about life in the army, and umpteen interviews.

At the end of the three days I was told I was going to be based at Strensall near York and that I was going into the Queens Lancashire regiment with a proud History going back as far 1689. It carried more battle honours on its colours than any other infantry unit in the Army. It was also able to proudly claim that it was the only regiment, from any army, ever, which had fought on every one of the World's inhabited continents.

The day had arrived Sean was coming along with me in to the Queens Lancashire Regiment. As for Dale he was going into the Kings Own Regiment. The coach was ready. I said my goodbyes to Dale. I was on my way to Strensall army barracks to do three years in the army or so I thought. I was nearly twenty years old and I would be twenty three when I came out of the army so I was still young enough to do the things I really wanted to do.

We arrived at Strensall army barracks in the late afternoon and as usual, we were stopped at the barrier by a soldier and then let through after our papers were found to be in order.

We were all taken into a large room and as usual we were be greeted by our block Lance-Corporal. I would later call him a bastard and that was the nick-name I used for him, while I served in the British army.

After being briefed we were shown to our sleeping quarters and beds were allocated so we knew where we would be bunking up.

We were also told the locations of the games room, the canteen etc. and the times we had our meals; also, what time we had to get up and what kind of training we were to receive and so on.

Getting up for breakfast was 6.15 and then back to barracks for a quick room inspection. Then we were out on parade at around 8.15 every day. All that did not go down too well with me.

I always looked forward to meal times and I have to say the British army food was excellent. You could eat as much as you wanted from sirloin steak, lamb, every meat you could think of and the same with the desert. There was every cake you could think of and the ice-cream was out of this world.

My sleeping quarters were similar to the ones I had slept in, in the French Foreign Legion. The only difference was that it was a lot more modern and cleaner and not as many beds in each barracks.

I settled in pretty quickly on the first night and got on well with most people.

The morning soon came. It was lights on at 6.15; tidy your beds and then stand by your beds.

The Lance Corporal would check all the beds and the sheets had to have no creases in and be nicely squared. This would happen every morning without fail. As the days past my bed was frequently tilted over and the Lance Corporal would scream in my face because it wasn't good enough.

Now and again I was forced to do press-ups until I got my bed right.

The day I was provided with all my army kit, my boots and my gym kit, I now felt like a real soldier and I did feel proud at the beginning.

The first six weeks were very much an introductory phase in the Infantry. They covered a multitude of subjects such as Values & Standards, Physical Training, and Skill at Arms lessons, drill and Field craft. This was a busy phase for me as recruits would remain in the barracks

It was very different from the French Foreign Legion. The British army was far more professional. You didn't get time to be bored as you were either doing interviews or gym work or physical training which I enjoyed very much.

I didn't see much bullying; only from the Lance Corporal who I called 'the bastard' with his big mouth. You had to be on your toes all the time with him.

The only altercation I had and it was only the once, was with a lad from Liverpool who was slagging me off because I was from Bolton. He gave me a little slap and I responded by punching him over his chair.

After four weeks we were allowed to have a night out but we were pre-warned about not upsetting the locals by chatting up the local girls. Also we must always stay in groups and not to walk back to base on our own. It turned out that many a soldier had had a good hiding from the locals; such were the bad feelings against us.

I always took advantage of my nights out enjoying the local girls company and I'm not ashamed to say I had a knee trembler on a few occasions on the way back to base.

I can honestly say it's true; girls do love a man in uniform.

On the odd occasion I had been drunk and depending on who was on barrier duty, we usually managed to get through without any problems. Whenever I did guard duty, I would return the favour.

I only ever got in trouble once while on guard duty. That was when I forgot to salute an officer. I paid the price. I was left in the hands of 'the bastard,' my block Lance Corporal who derived great satisfaction from making me clean his boots over and over again; hence the name 'bastard.'

And on various occasions, if my uniform was not up to scratch or my bed or my army boots, 'the bastard' would have the shiniest boots on the camp.

I was longing to visit my home town to see my friends and family and the chance came. I got a week-end leave.

When my mother saw me in my uniform she cried. She told me she was very proud and that I looked a changed man, all grown-up she said.

I went out on the lash (piss-up) with my friends. They were telling me what was going on in the football games and all the trouble Bolton had had with Blackburn and Burnley and it had hurt our team up and down the country.

The more beer I drank the more home-sick I became. I missed all the football and all the fun that was attached to it.

It started to sink in that I was missing my freedom. I was naturally rebellious and I hated been told what to do

I felt suffocated and I blamed my father for turning me into the person I was.

The beatings over the years had taken their toll on me. I wanted to be happy and to be free and to have fun; all the things my father wouldn't let me be.

The weekend passed quickly and now I had to go back in the army. I started to resent it but I still went back on time.

The training became more intense. I was being shown more about how to use a rifle in shooting practice on the shooting range.

I did a few days away on what they called adventure training. We went rock-climbing and did other activities. I started to feel so homesick that my run-ins with the Lance Corporal I called 'the bastard' became more frequent. I was fed with all the marching and the early 6.15 starts. Everything was getting on top of me. I had had enough. I had only been in the army eleven weeks; just a few weeks away from passing out.

I decided it's was time to go home. I signed the necessary papers and I bought myself out of the British army.

I was proud of what little time I had in the army and I was very proud to serve my country. But I was rebellious. I just couldn't hack being told what to do. All my younger days I wasn't allowed to have friends, or girl-friends. I didn't know what was right or wrong. I was brought up with violence and suffered so many times at the hands of my father.

I thought fighting and being in gangs was normal. I didn't realise at the time I was on a journey to the abyss.

Chapter ?????

Chapter seventeen

Bolton Wanderers - Home and away

I started going to football matches when I was as young as thirteen years old with my dad, following my beloved Bolton Wanderers.

I first saw trouble in 1973 in a night game at Burnden Park against Manchester City. There was a massive crowd of just over 43,000.

I ventured to the match with a few school friends. We didn't go into the game as we didn't have any tickets. We watched the game on a bridge at the back of the embankment.

The atmosphere was electric but my eyes weren't on the game for long. Outside the ground there was a large scale disturbance.

I watched with amazement as two sets of opposing fans ran in to each other with ferocity; fist and kicks were there a plenty. One lad was attacked with a bottle and was knocked unconscious.

It seemed to go on for ages until the police with dogs chased them off.

When the match finished we decided to leave as quickly as possible as we didn't want to get caught up in the aftermath. We made our way down the steps and round the back of the Lever End and onto Manchester Road. Then we heard a loud roar go up and the sounds that we would come to call Bolton aggro. The next thing, there were hundreds of Bolton supporters attacking Manchester City fans from all directions.

I lost my friends and I ran into a shop doorway to get away from all the trouble. It was a frightening experience but I was excited never the less.

Another game I went to was with my dad when Bolton played against Luton town in the FA cup in 1973; there were 39,000 present on that day. It wasn't the game that excited me; it was the large scale fighting at the Lever End. The trouble started when a large group of Luton fans came into the home end.

What stood out for me was that the Luton fans were dressed in orange boiler suits. I saw one lad with a dart in his head.

The Bolton fans attacked the Luton fans like a pack of wolves and punches and kicks were landing on the Luton fans heads and bodies from all angles. The Luton fans were chased out of the Bolton End and onto the pitch. A few of them were carried out on stretchers and some of them were badly beaten and lying unconscious on the terrace, covered in blood. After all the bravado that was the last game my dad would ever attend with me.

I started work when I was sixteen years old and I was on good wages. This gave me the opportunity to follow Bolton Wanderers home and away.

My first away game following Bolton Wanderers was a game against Blackpool our Lancashire rivals. On the morning of the game I set off with a few lads from Farnworth and we made our way to the train station. It was only 10am in the morning and there were hundreds of lads on the platform.

There were lots of older lads of all shapes and sizes. Some were skinheads, mods and rockers. After the troubles I saw at Bolton, I felt safe in their company.

The train journey only took an hour and every time we stopped at a station more lads got on the train. It was packed to the rafters.

When we arrived at Blackpool hundreds of lads piled off the train. The volume of noise was deafening; all you could hear was, "Bolton are back! Allo, Allo!!"

The police couldn't stop the masses of Bolton fans they just ran straight through them and ran down the road in their hundreds.

Shop windows were going through, all the way to the sea-front. I just followed them as I didn't want to be on my own. I never saw any large groups of Blackpool supporters and those few I did see were quickly dealt with and chased off.

The police were arresting anybody they could get hold of and I saw plenty put into police vans covered in blood. Along the front I saw a group of Blackpool fans outside a pub which was called 'The Manchester.' They were attacked from all sides and the pub was trashed.

After a while the police got control of the disorder and escorted us to the ground which was called Bloomfield Road.

Before we were let through the turnstiles the police searched us for weapons. I saw a few get arrested for having a variety of weapons; knuckle-duster, knives and sticks, hidden under their coats.

The Way End was packed to the rafters and there was only a fence separating us from the home supporters. Now and again you had to duck as bricks and coins were being thrown to and fro.

At half time I made my way down to the toilets but was stopped by the police. News was going round that a Blackpool fan had been stabbed to death near the toilets.

At the end of the game we were all held back. I was interviewed for over an hour because they took all our names and address.

They only let us leave two at a time which wasn't good news as there were hundreds of Blackpool fans lying in wait baying for our blood.

A lad who was much older me and I, then got chased for miles. I was lucky to escape without a serious beating. Quite a few of us suffered because of the death of a Blackpool fan.

On the way home I was very quiet. I was sickened by the serious violence and the death of a football fan. He was someone's son and would never now come home.

I didn't attend football matches for quite a while. I was put off by the death of a football fan. After all you don't deserve to die watching a game of football.

I was drifting in and out of relationships. The girls were all looking for something different and I always ended up going back to football as it was only my true passion.

One game that always stands out was in the 1977/78 season. It was a game at home against Nottingham Forest. I was getting a bit of a reputation then and I was accepted into the Bolton gangs. I was in the embankment expecting the Forest fans to be in our side of the ground.

There was a large commotion in the Lever End which was the Bolton end at the time. Forest fans had invaded the home end. There were large scuffles going on all over the Lever End.

I decided to invade the pitch with a few others and try to get across the pitch and into the Lever End. I was caught and arrested on the pitch and hand-cuffed, then frog-marched off the pitch to a chorus of boos from the home fans.

Little did I know that this was all witnessed by my mum, my sister and my brother? I was charged with the breach of the peace and later fined at the magistrates courts.

Anyway, after I arrived at my mother's house I was told that I was an embarrassment to the family and that I had to find somewhere else to live, as a punishment.

Over the years I was arrested for various offences but it still didn't stop me going to the matches.

Everton at home in a cup semi-final on a cold Tuesday night in 1976 was a much anticipated game. I was looking forward to it. After nearly getting my head kicked in with a good friend of mine, Amos, at their ground, it was time for revenge.

All day at work I was excited not just because we had a chance of going to Wembley, but a chance to mix it with the Scousers.

I finished work at 4pm and I got changed there, so I could make my way straight into town.

I started drinking early in the Trotters and by 6pm I was half drunk. It didn't help when I slipped going into the toilet and cracked my head on the wall which resulted in a small head wound with blood pouring down the side of my face.

I tried to wash it clean but the blood just kept pouring out. I had no choice, but go to a chemist and buy a bandage.

I just wrapped the bandage round my head to stop the bleeding and as I made my way back into town, I saw hundreds of Everton lads running towards the train station. There was a lot of shouting and screams. They were being chased by the Bolton supporters. One ran past me; big mistake I thought. Crack! I hit him so hard he fell on the floor. Revenge was sweet as my thoughts drifted back to the Everton away game when I was lucky to escape a beating.

All the way to the ground there were large scuffles. Word was getting round that an Everton fan had been thrown through a pub window. Police were baton charging Bolton supporters, to stop them attacking the Everton fans. There were literally hundreds of fans from both sides in a free-for-all.

Inside the ground it was electric. There were nearly 53,000 on that night with over 12,000 of them from Everton.

My head was really throbbing and the blood was still pouring down the side of my face. I was advised by a St. John Ambulance man to go for treatment in their first-aid room.

I walked round the pitch to cheers from the home fans as though I was some kind of hero who had been fighting for the cause. Little did they know that I fell over and cracked my head?

I received four stitches in my head wound and to make things worse, they rolled a bandage around my head.

I missed most of the match as there were long queues waiting to be treated. A lot of them had head wounds after being hit by missiles thrown from rival fans and they were covered in blood.

We lost the game 1-0 and the chance to get to Wembley. Outside the ground the Everton fans were celebrating.

There was a loud roar as hundred of Bolton's supporters attacked them with bottles and bricks. You could hear shouts of, "Bolton aggro, Bolton aggro!"

There were fans all over the floor covered in blood; police on horse-back charging into warring fans and plenty of sore heads in the morning after the police waded in with their batons.

Another game that stands out in my memory was Blackburn away, a night game in the 1977/78 season. It was a huge game as we needed to win to get promotion to division one.

Bolton was expecting to take nearly 20,000 supporters to Blackburn so I decided to leave Bolton early. I set off with a good few lads from Farnworth and arrived at the train station at noon. To my surprise there were already hundreds of lads on the platform and the match wasn't going to start till 7.45 pm in the evening.

The train had arrived on time but there were just too many of us. It was soon packed so we had to wait for the next one.

We finally arrived in Blackburn and there were already thousands of Bolton supporters walking about, singing and most of them were so drunk they couldn't walk.

All the pubs were packed with Bolton fans so a few of us decided to buy a few cans of beer and sit on the grass banks near the ground.

We tried to get into the Blackburn end but were turned away so we decided to go into the Bolton end. It was packed to the rafters. You couldn't breathe. We were packed in like sardines.

The ground was packed to the limit. There were thousands of Bolton fans all over the ground and the Blackburn end had been overrun with Bolton supporters.

Bolton won the game 1-0 and at the final whistle I invaded the pitch along with large numbers of others to celebrate our promotion to division one. I stayed in Blackburn till the early hours of the following morning celebrating and all you could hear in the pubs was the sound of champions echoing through the night.

I carried on following Bolton Wanderers home and away through the 70s and 80s all over the country. I was constantly getting into all kinds of trouble. I ended up in courts all over the country for various offences.

I had some fantastic memories following Bolton some good and some bad, but I did have some funny moments.

On the way back from a game at Derby our van stopped off at Matlock and Mick and I decided to go for a walk.

We saw two girls who were in their twenties sitting on a bench eyeing us up. So, we didn't want disappoint them and made our way over to them. We both asked them would they like to go somewhere for a cuddle out of sight of the passing public. We went behind an old building out of view. I was kissing this girl and I was just going to get down to the nitty-gritty when we heard police sirens. I knew straight away there was something wrong so I kissed her good bye and ran off, pulling my pants up.

Some of the Bolton lads who were in the van with us had robbed an arcade so it was time to get out of Matlock at speed.

I supported Bolton with a passion, home and away and all over the country. I made some fantastic friends over the years following Bolton. They were like a family to me. There were plenty of characters from all walks of life. One man was 'Fred Dickie.' He was a legend on the terraces and I was honoured to have known him. He was a true 'gentleman' and I always had huge respect for him.

I carried on following Bolton for the next few years and getting into scrapes all over the country, but it would all come to a tragic end as you will find out later.

Chapter eighteen

The Road to Oblivion

After signing myself out of the army, my life was at a crossroads. My mother was heartbroken and my father said he washed his hands of me.

I decided it was time to leave home for the final time. I ended up in a small bedsit on Bromwich Street in Bolton. It was not much bigger then my old box-room at my old house.

There was a small table and a bed; a small cupboard where I could store some food, a little fridge and a small wardrobe and that was it. I had to share the bathroom and toilet with all the other tenants.

I didn't have much money, I wasn't working, so I was restricted as to the things I was able to do. My mother still kept in touch with me and she still gave me money whenever I needed it and she even brought food down for me, which she did most weeks. My mother was always there for me. Once a week she would come down to my flat and give it a good clean.

My flat wasn't far from Burnden Park which was very handy to go to and watch my beloved Bolton Wanderers. I was still getting into trouble and ending up in the police cells, on various occasions.

I had some good fortune, however. I got myself a job in a pop factory called Cambrian Soft Drinks in Bolton. This pleased my mother no end.

The hours were from 8 till 4 so I had plenty of spare time for myself. I still met up at weekends with my friends and did the normal things; got drunk, mixed with the girls and took the occasional girl back to mine.

Life was pretty boring; it was just work, sleep and get drunk at the weekends.

Things did take a turn for the worse when I met up as usual with my mates after the game against Derby County. I was walking up Manchester Road with three of my mates towards town with the intentions of going there. Suddenly a large white Luton van pulled up next to us and the shutters opened. There was a loud chant and about fifteen Derby lads jumped out. My three mates did a runner and I was all alone to face the fierce barrage of punches and kicks against my body. My leather jacket was ripped apart and I was getting badly beaten. Only the police sirens saved me from a hospital visit. The Derby lads disappeared back into the Luton van and they were gone before the police arrived. I was black and blue and covered in blood. The police jumped on me and handcuffed me and pushed me into the back of the van. I was trying to plead my innocence but they just laughed and said you live by the sword and you die by the sword. I was taken to Bolton police station and charged with a breach of the peace. I had my finger prints taken and then I was thrown in to the cells.

It was there in those cells that I did a lot of hard thinking. I decided to turn my back on football violence for good. I was twenty four years old and pressing the self-destruct button. I wanted to be normal guy who went home to a wife and kids and had a happy family. Since I was four years old I had only ever seen violence; the abuse and the beatings, running away to Paris when I was fourteen years old and I had been running away ever since. I ran from problem to problem; the French Foreign Legion, the British Army. I decided I had to put it all to bed before I destroyed myself with self-pity. I was kicked out of the cells in the early hours and I caught a taxi and went straight home. I cleaned myself up and I promised to myself that I was going to turn my life around.

I decided to turn my back on football for good and I tried to avoid my friends whenever possible and the bars around Bolton town centre to avoid getting involved in any trouble.

Around 1984 I met a girl called Belinda in a bar in Atherton which is just outside of Bolton. I was standing at the bar and this girl was standing behind me. I noticed her straight away. She was very pretty, slim with short brown hair and very casually dressed. We just smiled at each other and started talking. We got on very well and had a good laugh and we chatted till the early hours. We started seeing each other on a regular basis and before long we both moved in together in a rented apartment. It was nothing special but homely never the less. My mother was very happy that I had turned my life around and turned my back on football and all the troubles that followed from it.

We travelled together as a couple for the first time to Croatia, to a place called Porec. This was one of the most visited towns in Croatia. It was popular with the British as well as most other Europeans. Porec was a lovely town with history stretching back two thousand years. In it were buildings and frontages from when it had been conquered and re-conquered throughout the centuries. There were several squares, some tiny, many small alleys and narrow lanes with buildings that seem to stretch forever upwards! We stayed for a week and walked around holding hands. This was a new experience for me. Drinking in the small bars next to the beautiful beach surrounded by the beautiful blue sea was a dream-come-true, for me. We strolled around the lovely old town with quaint, narrow, cobbled streets lined with bars, cafés and an interesting variety of shops. In the evening the streets were noisy and bustling with lots of people enjoying a meal or a drink, entertained by a variety of bands and musicians. The week passed by so quickly and then it was time to fly home. I had enjoyed our first holiday together. I really did care for her and Belinda cared about me. I wasn't madly in love with her but I felt contented in my life and I was very happy to be with her. My life had been turned around and I was very grateful to her for that. She showed me lots of love and caring which I had sadly missed in my life.

After a few years of being together we decided that the time was right to start a family but things didn't work out as planned. For two years we tried but nothing happened. We decided to see our doctor and voice our concerns. I went to see a specialist to have some sperm tests and other tests and I was given the all clear. Belinda was given some fertility drugs to help her conceive but even with the drugs nothing happened. This carried on for another year. We even went abroad to Germany a couple of times and Amsterdam to take our minds of things. The stress started to get to Belinda; she wanted children and our relationship started to suffer and eventually we started to grow apart. I was with Belinda for nearly eight years. I never regretted the relationship as she was a sweet girl who helped me through difficult times. She helped to heal the nightmares I used to have about my past abuse and beatings.

In March 1990 I received a phone call from my mother to say my father was seriously ill in hospital.

"I don't care," I told her. "He doesn't deserve any affection from me after the way he treated me." It was callous but nonetheless that was the way I felt.

"Please Ian," my mother pleaded. "Go and see him. If you won't do it for him, do it for me. Make peace with him before he dies."

When I arrived at the hospital my mother was already there. My father was in a side-ward, wired up to all kinds of monitors. I sat next to him and I actually felt sorry for him for the first time in years. He held out his hand and I held it. He mumbled something to me but I couldn't understand what he was saying. I just hoped that he was trying to say sorry to me. He held my hand tightly then peacefully slipped away. I suddenly felt the pain I thought I could never experience. I felt a sudden sense of loss and I was glad that I had made peace with him before he died.

I stood at his funeral looking at his wreath. Suddenly I felt an even stronger sense of loss and this totally confused me. I stood there deep in thought. All I wanted in life was to be loved and I had a father who found it difficult to show or tell me that.

I made a decision there and then to turn my back on all the troubles and try to turn my life around. I had been surrounded by violence right through my childhood and youth and I wanted to forget it all. I had been drifting through life being rebellious and part of that was my father's fault. If only he had given me love and attention, maybe I could have done things differently in my life.

His passing coincided with the failed relationship with Belinda and I decided to go on holiday and after that to try to sort my life out.

So, one day I decided to go into Bolton and book a holiday. I didn't care where it was as long as I got away. I stopped outside a travel-agent and saw a holiday to Corfu, advertised in their window.

This was the start of another journey which would change my whole life forever and my journey to the abyss.

Chapter nineteen

Falling in love with a beautiful stranger

It was a momentary decision. The thought came into my head to take the holiday in Greece. I'd always fancied going and Corfu was one of the Greek islands. It would be nice to get away to see the sights and also I thought it would be a bit of an adventure. Had I known this notion of a short break would turn out to be the longest and worst ordeal I was ever going to face; my decision might have been different. As it turned out, it took me down roads I certainly didn't want to go down. The only driving force that saw me through the hardest times was the love for my son and love can indeed move mountains. I later realised that was exactly what faced me.

Everybody has a tale to tell. I have met people whose lives have been remarkable and inspiring. I hope that this part of my story will be just as inspiring and illuminating for those who find themselves in a similar position to mine.

In 1990 I met a Greek girl, Helen, in Corfu. I only knew her for a few days, but I fell in love. I was deeply in love with her from the moment I met her. She was different from anybody I had ever known. She was so beautiful and caring, very loveable and fun to be with. At the end of the holiday, we said our goodbyes and I thought I would never see her again. The flight back to England was a quiet one. I was deep in thought and couldn't get Helen out of my mind.

After I had been home for three weeks, I received a letter from Helen inviting me to Athens and I willingly accepted.

I had already decided before I landed back in England that I was going back to Greece to be with Helen. I was originally going for just one week, but I stayed for five. Those five weeks were the best time of my life. Helen and I grew very close while we were together and during the last week when I was preparing to go home, she told her mother she wanted to go to England so we could be together. Helen was nineteen years old and her mother refused her permission to travel to England with me. I was under no illusions when her mother, Maria said to me, "You go back to England. Helen stays here."

I left the girl I loved with a broken heart. She was forced to stay in Greece under the watchful eye of her mother. She was almost a prisoner in her own home. Maria still considered Helen to be a little child. She wasn't allowed to wear make-up or to have boyfriends. I interpreted that to mean that she wasn't free to love and to have feelings.

I arrived in England alone on that fateful Friday morning and as crazy as it may seem, the following day, driven by love, I made a hasty decision to hitch-hike back to Greece. Within a couple of hours, I had packed and was ready to leave. I had no plan and very little money. I checked on how much money I had. It wasn't much - one hundred and eighty pounds in total. I just wanted to be with Helen and that's all I cared about. I didn't sleep much that night. I was thinking about how I was going to get to Athens with so little money, but come hell or high water, I was determined to do it.

All I knew was that I was going to go by coach to London and then by another coach to Dover. I would have to find my way across France and Italy before taking a boat to Greece. I didn't have the money for a flight so that was my only option. The journey to London was long, but uneventful and after a further two hour trip, I landed in Dover where I booked a single ticket on the ferry to Calais. I had taken enough food to last me for a few days. I didn't know how long I was staying in Greece or if I ever wanted to go back to England.

As luck would have it, I met a family from Bristol on the ferry. They were Julie, James and their children, Edward and Mark. They had a campervan and were aiming to travel through France to Milan, Italy. It was inevitable that they would ask where I was going and they were shocked that I would even attempt to hitch-hike to Greece. When I told them about Helen they understood my need. I simply wanted to be with her. I missed her so much and my life was empty without her.

"You must be crazy trying to hitch-hike all the way to Greece," they told me, "but if you like, you can come with us until we arrive in Italy. We aren't going as far as you need to go, but it will help you on your way."

"Are you kidding?" I asked in astonishment. "Thank you so much. I can't tell you how grateful I am."

It was a long trip, but very enjoyable. I was more than grateful for the food and a place to rest my head at night. I was in good company and we had interesting conversations. I saw some fascinating places, but I was getting fed up, because all I wanted to do was get to Greece and see my beloved Helen. However, it gave me a chance to stop worrying about Helen for a while and stop wondering what might be waiting for me when I arrived at her door. We arrived in Milan after driving through some memorable places – Reims, Dijon and Mont Blanc. After buying me a meal, the family drove me to the train station and paid for my ticket to Ancona where I could catch the boat to Greece. Julie had packed up some food and water for me to have on my travels. She and James were my guardian angels, that's for sure and I shall never be able to thank them enough.

It wasn't difficult to find the port in Ancona and soon I was on my way to Patras in Greece from where I would easily be able to travel to Athens. The voyage took twenty-three hours. In order to save money, I didn't book a cabin so I slept on the floor when it was possible to find a suitable space. The packed lunch that Julie had given me kept the hunger away so I didn't need to go to the restaurant. I sat on the top deck and watched the ocean as we sailed across the Adriatic Sea to my love.

From Patras, I set off on the relatively short trip to Athens. With every mile I travelled, I was becoming more and more nervous. I didn't know what kind of reception I would receive from Maria and her husband, Vangelis, but I knew Helen would be happy to see me. I needed to spend some time with her and see if we had a future together. Personally, I had already made up my mind that I wanted to spend the rest of my life with her, but common sense (I did have some even though my recent rash actions might not suggest that) told me we had to be together for a while. At that point, I didn't care if it were in England or in Greece. I convinced myself it was more than a holiday romance and I wanted to prove that to Helen's mother, Maria and step-father, Vangelis. I wanted to show them how much I loved Helen. If I had to live in Greece so be it. I knew I would have to find a job and a place to live to support Helen and make her happy. My intentions were honourable.

I took the green bus to Perama where Helen lived and was dropped off at the bottom of the hill near Helen's house. I sat down on a bench and took a deep breath. The

Athens August sun beat down on me, but I needed to collect my thoughts before I approached the house. I hadn't told Helen I was coming. I wanted to surprise her.

Every nerve in my body was jangling, but my time had to come to face Maria and Vangelis, so I started to walk slowly up the hill towards Helen's house. I was afraid; I admit it. I knew Maria and what she was like, but if my love for Helen meant anything at all, I had to prepare myself for what might happen. Helen was sitting on the balcony along with Maria, her mother. I saw them before I reached the front door at the top of the steps. Helen was shocked, but happy to see me, but her mother wasn't happy at all.

Maria stood at the top of the steps and harshly shouted down to me, "Go back to England!"

Helen came out and said quietly, "Wait for me at the cafe at the bottom of the road."

I waited in the cafe for over an hour and I was on my third bottle of beer, when Helen came rushing down the hill as if she were being chased by a pack of hounds. She had sneaked out to meet me. She was crying and I put my arms around her to comfort her. She felt so good in my arms and I melted at her touch, the feel of her body next to mine and the delicious scent of her. "I love you," I whispered. "I love you with all my heart and soul."

Gradually she calmed down, but she had to impart bad news. "You can't stay at the house. You are not welcome. My mother says our relationship is finished."

I looked into her eyes. "Do you still want me?" I asked earnestly.

"Yes, I do," she replied.

With that I took her into Piraeus, away from the clutches of her mother. We headed for the Alexandra bar where we used to go when I first went to Athens. We talked for hours, Oblivious to what was going on around us. I told Helen straight. "You must come to England with me. You can't stay here, not now. I want you to be free and live a normal life with me in England." We agreed that she would tell her mother she was going back to England with me the following morning.

We stayed out all night and slept on a park bench near her grandma's house. It wasn't cold; in fact it was quite warm even though the temperature of the night air was cooler. I held Helen in my arms all night and just stared at her. I was stroking her hair and looking forward to our being together not realising the full implications of the situation. When Helen awoke, she said she would go to her grandma's for some food and a drink. I was so tired and I slept on the bench while I was waiting for Helen to return. Suddenly, I was awakened by her granddad who slapped me across the face. He was shouting at me in Greek. I didn't understand what he was saying, but I knew he was very angry with me.

I jumped up and it was then I saw Maria and Vangelis rushing towards me with three other men I had never seen before. My heart was pounding in my chest. I was truly afraid of what was going to happen to me. Maria started to shove me and told me to go back to England. Then she kicked my suitcase over and slapped me. Helen sprang to my defence and started fighting with Maria.

The situation was manic. Vangelis attacked me, throwing punches at me from all directions. I had to fight back and I punched him a few times. The coward was lying on the floor screaming like a baby. The three Greek guys jumped on me like a pack of wolves. I couldn't escape. I was being punched and kicked all over the floor. My shirt tee shirt was ripped apart and my jeans were ripped. I was covered in blood. Helen was screaming and crying and shouting and then as suddenly as it had started, it stopped. Helen was pushed into a yellow taxi which belonged to Vangelis. I was forced into another taxi with the three Greek guys who had beaten me and I was taken to the police station.

When I arrived there Maria, Vangelis and Helen were already there. I was thrown out of the car along with my suitcase. Vangelis went into the police station. Within minutes a police officer came out and told me that Helen didn't want to go with me. "You must go home," he said.

I looked at Helen. She was in tears and was being held back by Maria and Vangelis. The officer then warned me, "If you don't go home, the family will kill you and I will turn a blind eye to it. We could find you dead on some piece of derelict land."

I had been in many scrapes in the past with the gang fights in Farnworth and football punch-ups on a Saturday afternoon following Bolton Wanderers in my earlier days, but this was on a different scale. I had to go back to England, otherwise I might be found dead on some derelict land like the officer had said and never be seen alive again.

I checked my pockets to make sure I had my passport and my wallet, but my wallet had gone. I must have lost it when I was fighting in the park. I shouted to Vangelis, "I have no money, but I have my passport. Vangelis smirked as he gave me fifty drachmas saying, "You must go back the way you came." Helen translated for me and Vangelis said, "You will be taken by car to Athens and put on a coach to Patras where you will go by boat to Italy and find your own way home."

Maria stepped forward and spoke to Helen in Greek. Helen translated again. "My mother says you can write to me. Don't worry, I'll be fine."

I gave Helen a hug. She kissed me goodbye then she was taken away. My heart sank and I was put into a taxi with the three Greek guys who were Vangelis's friends. When we arrived at the coach station, I was given my suitcase and they stayed to make sure I left on the coach. It was like a film with a bad ending. I was on the coach alone going back to Patras having to face the long, sad journey home. It had taken me nearly five days to get there and I had stayed in Greece for just a day and a night.

I arrived in Patras and the first thing I did was to clean up. My face was a mess. I had black eyes and bruises on my left cheek. I cleaned up all the blood and got changed. I booked my ticket for the sea trip to Ancona which I knew would take over twenty hours and then I had to face the prospect of the long journey home. I felt numb and utterly, utterly sad. I could see people staring at me assuming they knew I was involved in some kind of trouble with all the bruises on my face.

My funds were low. I had just enough money for the boat to Ancona. I was thirsty, hungry and depressed. I was battered and bruised, but my brain was still functioning. I decided to use the cuts and bruises to my advantage. I went to the lost property office on the ship and spoke to the person in charge. Luckily for me, he spoke English. I turned on the tears. With my emotions being in tatters, it wasn't difficult for me and I told him I had been mugged and my wallet had been stolen. He asked me where and when and I told him in Patras earlier that day. "Surely you can see from my bruises that I was badly beaten."

He picked up the phone and rang the purser's office to tell him the story. Within five minutes, the captain came to see me. He gave me a special card with his signature on it that enabled me to eat what I wanted, but no drinks were included and he instructed me that I must eat only at meal times. I ate like a king. I appreciated the offer of food and filled my tray up to capacity with food and plenty of water. When I arrived at the till, the captain was angry as he told me no drinks. I just turned on the crocodile tears again and he relented. I had put so much food on my tray so it would last for a couple of days. I knew I would need it for the long trek home. The sea journey was long and I couldn't sleep, but at least my belly was full. I felt a bit better even though I was sore all over from the beating I had been given. I stayed on the top deck and watched as the ferry took me further and further away from the girl I loved. I couldn't stop thinking about the way I had left her. I was heart-broken, but I determined that I was not finished. I was down, but I wasn't out. After all, I'm a Farnworth lad and I'm English. We don't give up that easily. We fight our corner until we win.

I arrived in Ancona and I thought, *my God, I'm thousands of miles from home.* The thought was scary, but I simply had to get on my way as best I could. I started to hitch-hike outside the port and when a car stopped, the Italian driver asked in broken English, "Where you going?"

"England," I told him with a smile.

"Ha ha, very funny!" he commented. "Come on, get in. I take you to my house."

Strangely, I didn't feel in any danger. I had just escaped with my life after the worst beating I had ever had, so getting into the Italian guy's car didn't faze me. "I'm Vittorio," he said introducing himself.

I tapped on my chest. "Ian."

We arrived at his house in a matter of minutes and he invited me in to meet his son, Alonso. He also had a daughter who wasn't there at that time. Alonso could speak English and he was very courteous with me. They welcomed me into their home, gave me a sumptuous meal of spaghetti and meatballs, stuffed tomatoes and rice, chips and salads, all washed down with Italian red wine. Vittorio showed me his beautiful garden and invited me to stay the night with them. I told Alonso what had happened to me in Greece and he translated for his father. We spoke until the early hours of the morning. Vittorio reached out and touched my hand and gave me a sympathetic look.

"You must fight for the girl you love and take her to England," Alonso said gently.

I smiled and nodded. "I can promise you," I informed him, "it will take a lot more than a few bruises to stop me getting the girl I love." I had a hot bath and went to bed. I lay awake for a while thinking that I would definitely be back in Greece, but next time I would have a plan of action.

The following morning Alonso told me his father would drive me to the train station and buy me a ticket to Milan. I was to do the return trip to the station where Julie and James had dropped me off just a few short weeks before. When I went into the kitchen, Vittorio's daughter was there and ironically, her name was Maria. However, this Maria was kind and beautiful, not at all like the other whom I preferred not to think about just then. After breakfast, we had to say goodbye.

As promised, Vittorio drove me to the station, bought my ticket for me and gave me money for food. I hugged him and thanked him. I felt humbled by his kindness. It just proves, no matter where you are from, there are good people in the world.

"Good luck," he said as he left.

I was stuck in Milan for four hours. I kept walking along the main roads out of the city hoping I would be able to hitch a lift. Eventually, while I was sitting on a bench near a petrol station, a wagon pulled over. The driver must have seen my suitcase and it was obvious I was hitch-hiking.

He pulled in next to me and then wound his window down. He shouted at me in broken English, "Where are going?"

Just like I answered Vittorio, I replied, "England."

He laughed and gestured to me to get in the wagon. I put the suitcase in the back and sat in the front with him. He showed me a map and pointed out to me where he was going - Reims in France. I put my thumb up to him to say that will be fine. It wasn't far from Paris and Paris was a lot closer to home.

It was an interesting journey to say the least. I couldn't speak Italian and his English left much to be desired. The journey took over thirteen hours as we stopped off a few times for something to eat and the driver kindly paid for the food. He didn't tell me his name, but I have to say, he was quite a character. He tried his best to communicate with me and he was a good company. We travelled through Switzerland, Basel, Strasbourg and then on to Reims which was my final destination with him.

He dropped me off on the motorway in the middle of nowhere. It was dark and I was becoming worried because it had been nearly four hours without a lift. Then my knight in shining armour came along. I saw a wagon heading in my direction and he pulled over next to me. And wonder of wonders, an English voice called out, "Where're you going, pal?"

I was so happy. I thought I had won the lottery. "England," I said again.

"Jump in. I'm going to London."

"God is on my side after all," I said to myself.

His name was Albert and he asked me where I had been.

"Greece," I told him. I didn't feel the need to elaborate at that point.

"Were you on holiday?" he asked.

I laughed. "I was only in Greece one day and one night and it had taken me nearly five days to get there."

He looked at me and raised his eyebrows confused. I decided to tell him what had happened in Greece. What harm could it do?

Albert listened and then said, "They're fucking animals them Greeks. You have to watch your back with them."

He was a wonderful character, was Albert. He told me a few stories about what happened on his travels. He told me once while he was asleep in his wagon in Rome, two guys tried to break into the back of his truck. When he confronted them, they pulled knives on him.

"What did you do?" I asked him.

"I ran like the wind back to the cabin, locked the doors and drove like a bat out of hell until I felt safe."

I tried not to laugh, but he burst out laughing himself so we had a good laugh together. Now and again my thoughts would drift back to Helen and the trouble on the park, but I knew I had been lucky to get out of Greece alive. Next time I had to plan it properly and not just go to Greece on a whim.

The trip with Albert was a pleasant and memorable one. We arrived at Dover and then on to London where he dropped me off at a good point on the motorway to give me a better chance of a lift home.

Three or four lifts later, I was in Manchester – home territory- and only a bus ride home to Bolton. I had never been so pleased to see my house. I was so tired, mentally and physically and all I wanted to do was sleep. After a good night's sleep, I got up the following morning eager to start planning my next trip to Athens. I intended to end Helen's nightmare and bring her to England once and for all.

Chapter twenty

Passport to freedom and the magic bus

After I settled back into my routine in England, I started my plan to get Helen out of Greece. My first job was to start saving as much money as possible. I had already experienced travelling with very little money and it wasn't easy. I went to the local library to study maps of Greece and plan the best route for our escape. Escape seemed to be a drastic word, but knowing what Helen's family was like, I knew it would be like escaping from jail. In the meantime, I was writing to Helen every day saying how much I loved and missed her and this went on for a weeks.

Out of the blue, I received a letter from Helen saying she loved me and missed me and that she was sorry for what her family had done to me. *'Why are you not writing to me?'* she wrote. It didn't take a super brain to realise that Maria must have been intercepting my letters and probably having them translated. I decided not to tell Helen my plans to get her out of Greece, or when I was going there. I would make sure Maria knew nothing of my plans, but it meant I had to keep everything secret from Helen too. I continued writing letters to Helen telling her I loved her and missed her and what my life was like in England. As far as Maria was concerned, they were just love letters, but then in one of them, I put in something about Maria and I called her 'a fucking camel.' When Maria intercepted the letter, she was enraged and confronted Helen, telling her what I said. My plan had worked and Helen knew her mother had been opening her letters.

I received another letter from Helen that confirmed her mother was indeed intercepting her mail and having the letters translated. Helen gave me her friend, Valerie's address, but I had to use a different surname, 'Valerie Black' so Valerie would know the letters were from me. I continued to write to Maria's address too so that she wouldn't become suspicious. It was becoming like a military operation to get Helen out of Greece.

Gradually, I formulated my plans. I would to fly to Greece and stay for a week, but then travel back by coach with a company called Magic Bus. The Magic Bus was very famous in the nineteen-seventies as a no-frills cheap way to travel around Europe. The trip would take four days through Greece, Yugoslavia, Austria and Belgium. We would catch the ferry to Dover and then finally to London either by train or coach. I decided this was the safest route out of Greece for us. I knew if and when I got Helen, they would be waiting for us at the airport and the ferry port at Patras - the route I had taken after my last trip to Athens. I knew it was dangerous, but when you are in love, you do crazy things. I even bought some clothes to go out in disguise by wearing a cap, dark glasses to hide my face and to dress like the local Greeks by wearing jeans and a light coloured shirt so as not to make it too obvious that I looked like a tourist. Like I said, when you are in love, you do crazy things.

The day before I was due to leave, I went to see my mother and step-dad. I thought I owed it to them to tell them what I was up to. My mother was very concerned for my safety, but I told her not to worry as I had been planning it for weeks. I spent a short while with them and then I said my goodbyes.

I didn't sleep much during the night. I was thinking about the dangers I might face in Athens, but I had to put bad thoughts out of my head and just concentrate on getting Helen out of Greece. I have to admit I was frightened, not just of her family, but also in case I was unable to see her. However, when morning came, I was ready to go. I was travelling light deliberately in case I had to make a run for it. I arrived at Manchester Airport, checked in my case and as I walked through Passenger Control I thought, No turning back now, Ian.

I slept for most of the four hour flight with the help of a sleeping tablet my mother had given me. It stopped me from anticipating what might happen when I arrived at Helen's door. When we landed in Athens, I retrieved my case quite quickly and headed for the exit. I was on the look-out all the time as I going to the bus station. I knew Vangelis and his friends were taxi drivers and did regular airport runs.

I managed to take the bus to Piraeus without being seen, but I needed to find a hotel quickly in case any friends of Helen and her family were around. I was very nervous especially every time I saw a yellow cab. I tried to make sure I was surrounded by people so I couldn't be easily detected. I found the Ionian Hotel on a side street. I felt it would be better for me and out of sight from the main thoroughfare.

I quickly unpacked and went for something to eat, all the time keeping a watchful eye on anyone whom I might recognise. My main concern was making sure I wasn't seen. I waited until dark and then I caught the bus to Perama. I got off at the bottom of the hill and waited at the cafe where Helen and I used to drink. Helen had to pass by me if she was going out anywhere. I was drinking coke deliberately to keep a clear head. I didn't want to drink beer. I needed to keep my wits about me. As time passed, Helen was nowhere to be seen. By eleven-thirty it was time for me to go before the last bus left. I got out of the village as quickly as possible, because most of the residents knew me. I was on tenterhooks in case of recognition and I only felt safe when I was back in my hotel.

I did the same thing again the following day and still I didn't see Helen. On the third day I started to panic. I had only a few days left. I had to see her soon otherwise I would have to go back to England without her. I made my way to Perama and did the same thing I had done each day before. I waited in the cafe bar again. At about half-past nine, I saw Helen walking down the hill. My chance at last! I was just going to shout to her when I saw a yellow taxi pass the cafe and Vangelis was driving. Instinctively, I put my head down with my cap over my face. My heart was pounding and I was shaking with fear. I was petrified of being caught, but I was sitting close to the road so Helen had to pass close by me.

When she came near I called her name. She stopped and stood in front of me just staring. I didn't know if she was in shock or if she didn't recognise me. I called out her name again and when I took off my cap and dark glasses, she came straight to me. I held out my hand. She took it and she held on tightly. I left the cafe and I held her tight. She was crying with happiness, but I was very much aware that we had to get out of Perama quickly before we were seen together. We hid in an old building off the main road. Out of sight of the world, we held each other, kissed passionately and cried together. I wanted to take her to England and come hell, or high water, I would do just that.

"Do you want to come back to England with me?" I asked longingly.

"Yes, I do," she told me earnestly.

I hugged her tight and I held her in my arms for a few minutes, savouring the moment.

I told her my plans and that we weren't flying back or going via Patras to sail to Ancona. Those were the first places Vangelis would start looking for us. "We need to travel by coach. Trust me, I have it all planned."

I had to leave, but I told Helen to meet me in my hotel and wear two sets of clothes for the next few days. That way, she would have clothes to take with her. She needed to get her passport, an absolute necessity to get out of Greece. She was fearful of being seen with me as she knew something bad would happen to me if her family caught us together. I reassured her that if we were careful, we would be fine. I kissed her passionately again before I left. She waved to me and left under the cover of darkness.

I walked to the bus stop, caught the bus back to Piraeus and went straight to my hotel. I slept through the night knowing that soon I was going to be with Helen.

The following day, I waited in the hotel for her. When I heard a knock on my door, I was nervous and fearful that Helen had been caught and it would be Vangelis and his cronies. I was in no doubt that in round two, they would finish me off. My fears turned to happiness and relief when I saw it was Helen. I hugged and kissed her. Suddenly, she started to undress and as she took off her clothes she revealed another set underneath. I grinned at her and said, "Well done, my Greek princess! My plan is working." She did the same the next night and afterwards, she gave me her passport. I was delighted that she had been able to smuggle it out of the house without being caught red-handed. We made love for a couple hours which had the desired effect of calming us both down. The next day was judgement day if we were going to get out of Greece safely.

We spoke briefly about that fatal day on the car park. She told me she would never forgive her mother and Vangelis for what they did to me. I told her not to think about it as we still had to get out of Greece.

"Perhaps you had better go home now before your mother starts phoning your friends to find out where you are," I advised her. "We don't want anything to go wrong now that we have come so far. Be here at ten o'clock in the morning. Don't be late, or I will have to catch my coach back to England without you and I don't think I could bear not having you with me." I hugged her and smiled at her affectionately. "Good luck for tomorrow and be extra careful not to get caught otherwise this will be our last chance of being together."

I watched her through the window as she left. My head was swimming with thoughts that it might be the last time I would ever see her. "Please God; let it all go to plan."

I waited till dark and went out for something to eat. I thought a couple of beers might calm my nerves. I covered my movements by going into the side streets thinking, *Out of sight, out of mind*. I looked around at all the places in Piraeus where Helen and I did our courting. Even though they were very fond memories, I was still glad to be leaving it behind. Once back in the hotel, I felt safe, but I didn't sleep a wink. I was more scared than ever, not of the beatings I received just a few months ago, but of Helen not turning up.

I woke up with a start. It was twenty past nine the following morning. I must have drifted off to sleep and Helen was due in half an hour. My adrenaline was going and I could hardly breathe. My nerves were on edge, my knees were shaking and it was now ten o'clock. Every minute seemed like an hour. Twenty past ten and I was counting every nervous minute, every frantic second. At ten-thirty- nine Helen still wasn't there.

I started to panic. What if she isn't coming; what if she's been caught? Then there was a knock on the door. I froze. What if it was Vangelis and his cronies? What if Helen has been caught? I opened the door... it was Helen. I held her as if I had lost her and found her again. I can't describe my relief that she was actually there. All kinds of emotions were running through my mind, but I had to pull myself together. These were my plans and I didn't want to make any mistakes now.

We found the travel company office near to the bus station. We booked two single tickets to England on the infamous Magic Bus. The clerk told us the time of departure and explained the route.

"How long will it take?" I asked.

"It will take four days to arrive in London," she told us. "You will need your passports. May I see them, please?"

When she inspected Helen's, she looked up and said, "You will need a visa to travel through Yugoslavia."

My heart sank. "Where do we get a visa?" I asked anxiously. It was a major problem in that Helen needed a visa to travel through Yugoslavia and we needed to overcome that if we were ever going to get to England.

The ticket clerk was very helpful. "Don't worry. Go to the Yugoslavian Embassy in Athens and they will give you a visa. You must go now, because the Embassy will close in two hours. You have time, but remember the coach leaves at four-thirty."

I told Helen not worry. We had to risk getting a taxi. She was frightened in case Vangelis or any of his friends caught us. "We'll be very careful," I told her, "but we have no choice. We'll have to risk it; otherwise we won't be back in time to catch the coach."

We spotted a taxi driver buying some cigarettes at a kiosk and I asked Helen if she knew him. When she shook her head, I said, "Come on! Quick!" and then to the taxi driver, "Are you free?"

"Yes," he replied. "Where to?"

He took us to the Embassy and outside there were hundreds of people in long lines waiting to be seen. My heart dropped and I said out loud, "We have to get a visa now or we'll miss the coach." As the words came out of my mouth, I noticed a side door open and a security guard came out. I took Helen's hand and said," This is our chance. You speak to him in Greek. Tell him a sob story; say my father died; anything at all that will help us jump the queue and tell him our coach is leaving in an hour."

Helen worked her magic. To my relief, he let us in. I hugged him and kissed his cheek. I didn't give a damn what it looked like, I was just so happy. We quickly obtained Helen's visa and sped back to the coach before we missed it. The biggest problem now was to get to the coach before the family caught up with us. I knew they would be all over the place looking for us as they had family friends who had taxis and they would stop at nothing to track us down.

We got there with twenty minutes to spare and went to find the Magic Bus. 'Infamous' was the word I used previously and it was indeed only the word to describe it. The windows were filthy and cracked; there were cigarette ends all over the floor. There was no toilet and the back of the coach smelled like a sewer. Helen and I were disheartened. The other passengers fitted the brief perfectly. They were either hippies or students who were smoking marijuana, but we had no choice so we jumped on the coach and hugged each as tears ran down our faces. We had finally made it.

When the coach pulled out of Piraeus, we started out on what promised to be an incredible journey home. I sat back and tried to relax. I was thinking of Maria and Vangelis who would probably be worried about Helen by then and would definitely be searching for her at the airport and at Patras. Maria must have known Helen was with me if she had found out that Helen's passport was missing. I wouldn't feel safe until we reached the Yugoslavian border.

We slept intermittently as we were both mentally and physically drained. Helen slept in my arms she was totally worn out. We sat near the back of the bus near a group of lads from Rochdale. Rochdale isn't a million miles from my home town, so I found an affiliation with them. As we approached the Yugoslavian border control, I sensed something unusual was happening. Two Yugoslavian policemen came on board and started to check all the passports. That in itself wasn't strange, but they were armed to the teeth with guns and they looked very intimidating. When it came to our turn, we handed over our passports and I was petrified when he looked at Helen's. I was shit scared! If Maria had reported her missing, we were in deep trouble. The policeman stared first at me, then at Helen. My heart was beating wildly in my chest and I tried desperately not to let the fear show on my face. We waited in silence and then the anguish was over. They returned our passports and walked to the next seat.

Suddenly there an argument with some of the Rochdale lads, but I was too scared to turn round in case the police thought we were travelling together. The last thing I wanted was any problems with the Yugoslavian police. Two more policemen came on to the coach and walked to the back. The next minute, three of the Rochdale lads were arrested and taken of the coach in handcuffs. I had no idea what was going on, but after a short while the coach was allowed drive over the border and we were on our way. Once we were out of Greece, we just held each other close and breathed a sigh of utter relief. Giving her a kiss, I said, "Now, we are free! That's the first step on our road to freedom."

After a while, we got to know the Rochdale lads who were still on the coach. They informed us that the three lads who were arrested had been caught with drugs on them. In spite of that, they were all fun to be with and most were in the early twenties and all were characters in their own right. I grew friendly with a lad called Jimmy. He seemed to stand out from the rest. He was constantly talking about football violence and the things he used to get up to on his travels following Manchester United. When I told him I hated Manchester United with a passion we might have crossed swords with each other at some point when we were following our football teams, he asked who I supported.

"Bolton Wanderers," I replied and he laughed.

"I remember going to Burnden Park," he said still laughing. "It was always a dodgy place to visit."

I laughed with him although I couldn't imagine why Burnden Park would be considered dodgy. It was always a lovely, homely ground. I asked Jimmy what his friends were into in Rochdale.

"Mainly drugs and robbing shops," he said matter-of-factly, "and women," he continued with a wink.

I could see Helen wasn't interested in anything Jimmy had to say, so I ended the conversation with him by making the excuse that Helen wasn't well. We stopped off at various places along the way, some interesting; some not, but the breaks did take our minds off things and it gave us the opportunity to stretch our legs. We drove through Switzerland which was very beautiful and picturesque and then Austria. We stopped in Brussels in Belgium where we had a four hour break.

Brussels was awe inspiring with each surrounding building having unique architectural patterns I had never seen before. Helen and I decided to do a bit of sightseeing around Brussels main square as we had plenty of time on our hands. The coach park was close to the square so we didn't have to walk that far. There were charming sidewalks, cafés, shops and restaurants. Helen wanted to go window shopping which we did to pass the time. While we were walking round the shops, we bumped in to Jimmy and his friends.

"Do you want to come for something to eat?" he asked. "We can find somewhere and have a drink."

I thought it would do no harm so we followed them in to a cafe where you could smell strong coffee and local fish delicacies. Helen and I sat at a separate table and the Rochdale lads sat at two other tables as there were ten of them in all. I picked the menu up and was studying the prices. Everything was very expensive, too expensive for me to buy for us both. I knew Helen was hungry and I wanted her to eat. I pretended I had stomach ache and that I couldn't eat much so as not to embarrass myself by not being able to pay the extortionate prices and to make sure Helen had something to eat.

I ordered two coffees and some ham sandwiches for Helen, but I was distracted by the waiters taking lots of drinks and food to Jimmy and his friends. The beer was flowing and they were having a banquet. When I caught Jimmy's eye, he winked at me with a large grin on his face, indicating all the food was on the house. I presumed they didn't have the money to pay for it made me feel very uncomfortable. We left the cafe unnoticed by Jimmy and his friends. We didn't want to witness what would happen when they couldn't pay the bill and we decided to make our way to the coach. As we were walking back, we heard voices behind us. Two of the lads, Mick and Mark had left the cafe as things were getting out of hand. They had sensibly decided to leave.

We hadn't been back in our seats for long, when we heard police sirens. We looked through the coach windows and saw Jimmy and the rest of the Rochdale lads being chased by the police. More and more police arrived in the square and soon the lads were all arrested, handcuffed and put into the waiting police vans.

There were plenty of empty seats at the back of the coach but I have to say, the journey wasn't the same without Jimmy and his Rochdale friends. Helen, who hadn't been impressed with their antics, called the Rochdale lads hooligans. In spite of their being what I would call a rum lot, they had kept us amused during the long journey. The coach set off for Calais, our next stop. It was time to rest. I was tired after the long journey and all excitement.

We arrived at Calais, our final destination before we boarded the boat and sailed across the English Channel to England. There was yet another incident with one of the remaining two Rochdale lads. We had changed drivers and the new driver was Greek. I knew there would be problems as Greeks do not like any kind of unsociable behaviour. Unfortunately, Mark was smoking a joint and he was laughing as he was urinating on the back seat. I could see the driver looking through his rear view mirror. Helen was disgusted and I had to convince her all English people were not like that. When the coach stopped at the port, the driver got out and complained to the French police and Mark was escorted off the coach and put into a police car.

Soon we boarded the ferry after our passports had been checked. When we were getting off the coach, Mick whispered to me that when we were in English waters, he would sort the Greek driver out. Once on board, Helen and I headed to the bar. I reckoned I deserved a small beer after all the incidents we had witnessed on our journey. We were chatting when the Greek driver came in, bought a coffee and sat down. Suddenly, Mick, the last of the Rochdale lads ran up to him and knocked him off his chair, knocking him out cold.

It was almost as if Helen couldn't bear any more of the shenanigans and she promptly fainted. I was helping her recover while members of the crew jumped on Mick and frog-marched him out of the bar. I took Helen on deck to get some fresh air and we could see Dover in the distance. I hugged Helen and whispered, "Soon we will be on English soil and be free." I held Helen in my arms as I stared at the ocean waves. There is something mysterious about staring into the deep waters of the sea. I started to reflect on what had happened in the past few weeks and after all the heartache and tears, love had triumphed in the end. We landed at Dover and we both walked down the steps onto English soil. I turned to Helen and held her close. "I love you, my Greek princess. Now you are free."

Amidst my happiness, I saw Mick being escorted off the boat by two police officers. I smiled to myself and shook my head slowly. It was the end of interesting and eventful journey, but for Helen and me, it was the beginning of a new one.

When we arrived in Bolton I took Helen to meet my mother and my step-father Jack. There was an immediate rapport and they insisted that we stayed that first night in their home.

Chapter twenty one

I finally married the girl of my dreams

The following day, we didn't wake up until ten o'clock. We were totally refreshed and after saying goodbye and thanks to my mother and my step-dad, Jack, we were on our way to Alder Street, Great Lever where we would make our new home and our new life together.

Alder Street was a cobbled street of pre-war terraced houses, on each side. The house I lived in was a two-up, two-down house and it belonged to a housing association. It was very modern inside, very spacious with a large front room and modern kitchen. Upstairs were two good sized bedrooms and a small bathroom. It was adequate and it was my home, our home and I intended to make Helen happy there. I guess this is where the story really begins.

I opened my front door and carried her over the threshold as though we were just married. Unfortunately, it turned out to be a bit of an embarrassment as I fell over, unceremoniously dropping Helen on the floor and smashing a Greek vase. Naturally, Helen was a bit shaken, but she burst out laughing. I hoped this was not a sign of things to come. I didn't want to think we were already cursed with bad luck.

When I showed Helen round the house, she was delighted. "It's a lovely house," she said happily. "I like it and I'm going to be happy here with you."

She settled down very quickly. As the days passed by I took Helen around Bolton town centre. There was a great range of high street names and independent retailers, places to eat and relax. I took to her to the museum as I knew she would enjoy it as she loves history and she really enjoyed the Egyptian Exhibition.

I introduced her to all my friends and took her out whenever possible to help her settle in quickly and enjoyably. The weeks flew by and I was so happy in my life. I was so much in love with her and she obviously was with me. I told her almost every five minutes that I loved her. I just couldn't stop holding Helen in my arms. I had never been so happy. She was so beautiful. I had crossed land and sea to be with her. I had been beaten by her Greek family and forced to leave Athens. I had returned secretly and smuggled her out of Greece and I would do it all again. Such was the love I had for Helen. All the anger and the hatred had gone when my father died. It was a new beginning for me; a new chapter in my life and I wanted to shout out loud and tell the whole world how much I loved her.

About eight weeks after we had arrived, she began to feel unwell so I took her to the doctor's. He asked her a few questions about her symptoms and then he examined her, requesting her to provide a urine sample. When she went back into the surgery, he told her he would have to send the sample off to the lab. I was worried there might be something seriously wrong with her, but the doctor informed us, "I think you might be pregnant." I was in total shock.

"She can't be!" I said. "I was in a previous relationship for eight years and nothing happened. We have only been together for a few weeks."

The doctor smiled. "Every relationship is different." I looked at Helen and she was as white as a sheet. We left the doctor's and walked home. It was not very far and Helen didn't speak a word. When we arrived home, she just put her arms around me and started to cry. I held her in my arms until she was calm. I was in shock too, but the truth of the matter was, I was actually very happy about it. I felt I couldn't show this to Helen as I didn't know what kind of reaction I would get. Looking back, I thought Helen was afraid because her mother used to do everything for her. In Greece, she wasn't allowed to do even the simplest things such as ironing, or washing dishes. She was totally under the control of her mother even in things like not being allowed to wear make-up. Her mother had treated her like a child all of her life. She hadn't been allowed to have boyfriends but it was all behind us now.

After the initial shock at the doctors that Helen might be pregnant the day had arrived when we would find out the results from the lab. The phone rang. It was the doctor. He spoke cheerily. "The results are here and it's positive. Congratulations!"

The feeling was incredible. I was going to be a father! It was the happiest I had ever felt in my whole life. It was unreal and I said to myself, "My life is going to change forever."

The troubles I had in the past were long gone. I went upstairs and told Helen. "You are going to be a mother!" She burst into tears and put her arms around me. This time they were tears of joy. I rang round all my family, bar my mother and Jack whom I wanted to tell in person. I knew they would be happy with such good news. I decided to go and see them on the same day we had the pregnancy confirmed. I had bought a bottle of champagne the day before. We took a taxi to my mother's house and I had butterflies all the way there. I was so excited to be telling her the brilliant news. When we arrived, we sat in the kitchen and my mother knew straight away I had something to tell her as I couldn't stop smiling. I allowed Helen to break the news as her English was now very good. My mum and Jack were so happy; they jumped up from their chairs and hugged us both fondly. I looked at Helen and she was really happy. I was very proud of her and I thought she now had a real family who would love her for who she is; a kind, generous and loving girl who had so much love to give. We stayed with Mum and Jack for most of the day and celebrated.

With the news of her pregnancy confirmed it felt the right time and so I got down on one knee. "Helen, will you marry me?"

Helen looked into my eyes and lovingly said, "Yes." I wanted to tell the whole world that I was going to be a father and I was getting married. I was absolutely ecstatic.

The next four months were spent planning our wedding day. I took Helen into Bolton and walked round the jewellery shops looking for a wedding ring. Next we bought clothes. I found a smart jacket, shirt and tie and Helen bought a purple dress in a size which would disguise her four months baby bump. Over the coming weeks, we ordered the wedding cake and booked everything necessary to give us a wonderful wedding day.

On the morning of the wedding in February 1991, I hugged Helen and told her I truly loved her. "Thank you for turning my life around. I would go through all the heartache in Greece again to bring you here. You are the love of my life."

She looked so beautiful with her long beautiful blonde hair. She had a lovely lilac dress covering her small bump as she was now a few months pregnant. Holding her wedding posy of white coronations she then told me, "We are we ready now."

I smiled, "The car is here now Helen." We were taken to the Bolton Registry Office. Outside were my mum and Jack and few members of our family and friends.

Before we were married I gave Helen a red rose like the one I had given her in Corfu. We then walked into the room with the music of Two Hearts in the background. That was the song I had chosen for her in Corfu and then we took the wedding vows and became man and wife. I hugged her tightly and thanked her for changing my life I cried with tears running down my face. I thanked her for making me so happy for the first time in my life. I promised her I would love her forever. I had finally married the girl of my dreams.

That night we celebrated till the early hours and we made love like no other time. She fell asleep in my arms with a smile on her face. She was finally free from the grasp from her mother and now she was mine forever, or so I thought.

The Happy Couple

Chapter twenty two

The birth of Christopher

It was a wonderful time being married and Helen being pregnant was the happiest time of my whole life. I just couldn't believe this was happening to me. I looked back at the abuse and the things I used to get up to; it was now a thing of the past. I had come a long way and I was a changed man. I was married to the most beautiful girl in the world.

Every night throughout her pregnancy Helen used to put my hand on her bump so that I could feel the baby moving. I used to laugh and say with a huge smile, "You're only a few weeks pregnant you must have indigestion."

But as the months went on it would be something I would do with excitement and joy. The first scan at the hospital was very exciting. We couldn't see much at the twelve weeks but it brought realisation that I was going to be a father.

We started to buy things for the baby; nappies and unisex baby grows as we didn't know the sex of the baby yet. But as the weeks past by it was soon time for Helen to have her second scan and we would then know the sex of the baby.

We found out that Helen was going to have a baby boy. The tears started to flow I was happy but emotional. We both decided to call him Christopher. The reason was because after I was beaten and forced to leave Athens and was hitch hiking home, I found a Saint Christopher. I kept it as I thought it would bring me good luck; a kind of lucky charm. So our new baby son had to be called Christopher.

Helen was so happy and contented. She was buying baby clothes nearly every day and my family was always calling in with things for the baby. We went to a baby shop and we bought a pram. Realisation was sinking in now that I was going to be a father. I was so proud and so excited I just couldn't wait for the birth of my son.

I started to decorate the baby's bedroom. We decorated the bedroom with blue wallpaper with yellow pictures of animals. Each week we would buy things for Christopher's room; a cradle, a cot and things to match the wallpaper.

His room was so beautiful. All we needed now was the baby and then it would be complete. Helen's bump was getting bigger by the day and she was getting more tired and the sickness was getting worse day by day. I started to read baby books and studied what the baby would have looked liked in the womb as he developed. We both used to laugh and say he's gone from being a prawn to a bigger fish; it certainly was an exciting times for us both.

She was now nearly eight months pregnant and we started to visit the hospital more often. Helen was getting bigger and bigger and I used to pull her leg about it but she took it all in good fun.

Then it happened. In the early hours of the morning Helen said she was getting contractions. I said you can't be; you still have three weeks to go. She was crying with the pain and said to go and ring for an ambulance. I ran down stairs and in my haste I slipped and banged my head against the wall.

I rang the hospital and I was panicking as well as having a lump on my head. They were asking me how often the contractions were coming. I said frequently, I think. The ambulance was on its way. I quickly packed her things. The ambulance arrived after only a few minutes.

In the hospital they did some tests on her and they told us that she had to be induced Helen looked shocked. Secretly, I was pleased as the baby would be early. I left the hospital in the early hours. I went back the following day and Helen was still being induced but she looked comfortable with the situation. My mother was even more excited than me and she kept ringing the hospital ever five minutes. Nothing happened all day although she was still getting contractions.

I kissed her good night and left the hospital and went home to get some rest. At 11:45 the phone rang. It was the nurse. She told me that Helen was in labour. I dashed back to the hospital. It was only ten minutes from my house. At 12:45 they took Helen down to the delivery suite and exactly at 1 o'clock Christopher was born.

The first time I held him I cried. I was so happy. He looked so small in my arms. He just looked like a baby doll. I gave Christopher back to Helen and I went to the toilet. I broke down and cried. My thoughts went back to my father; why couldn't love me like I loved my son? Why did he hurt me the way he did?

I had to pull myself together and get back to Helen. I had son and I promised myself that I would love him forever and I would never hurt him like father did to me.

Helen stayed in hospital for two days and I made sure the nursery was ready for when my son came home.

I visited her in hospital and I took a blue balloon with, *congratulations a baby boy* printed on it. I also took flowers. I couldn't wait to hold Christopher again. My mother and Jack brought Helen and the baby home.

It was an exciting times for us both. Helen struggled at first with Christopher so I used to change his nappies and feed him. I used to enjoy it.

Then I made the momentous decision that we should tell Helen's mother that we were married and had a baby boy. Helen was very reluctant as she has not spoken directly to her mother for almost a year, not, in fact, since that fateful day I smuggled her out of Greece. The only communication she had had with her mother was to write to her tell her she was safe in England and that she was living with me, the man she loved and wanted to spend her life with. Helen made sure that she didn't put our address on the letter. We didn't trust her mother, or any other members of her family. We didn't want them to follow us and come to England to reap their revenge.

It was my decision that Helen should tell her mother. I just wanted to put my differences to one side even though I could never forgive her for trying to destroy our relationship. Nor could I forgive her for the beating I received. That said, the day came when Helen plucked up the courage to phone. She was very nervous and very afraid, but she phoned her mother nevertheless. I could literally feel the tension between them. There was a lot of shouting and screaming which went on for a good twenty minutes and then Helen put the phone down. I asked what had happened, and what her mother had said to her. I felt so sorry for Helen. She didn't deserve the way Maria treated her. She was distraught. She sat down and started to cry. I held her in my arms to comfort her. She was heartbroken and she trembled as I held her close. She had tried to make peace with her mother and all she had received in return was grief. She eventually told me what her mother had said. In a low voice she explained.

All my family and friends, as well as the police had been looking for us all night when I went missing with you. They scoured Athens. Her mother and Vangelis even went to Corfu.

"Why did they do that?" I asked unbelieving.

"Because that's where we met and they thought that's where we might go," she told me. "I don't think they could believe I was in England. It is so far away from Athens." It was apparent that her family had taken drastic steps to find us but without success. Helen was twenty years old and they still wanted her to be tied to her mother's apron strings. Things like that should not be happening in the twentieth century. It was strange to me that they hadn't traced us through the ports of exit and entry during our travels. We had used our passports after all, but I realised I was very lucky to escape with my life.

Helen was my responsibility now and I would protect her with my life if needs be. That night we reminisced about much of what had happened to us in the past year. It brought back bad memories of Greece when I first visited Helen in June 1990, when I wasn't allowed to kiss her, or even hold her hand.

I remembered on one occasion when Helen and I were kissing like most couples do outside the train station in Piraeus, one of her step-dad's friends saw us and phoned her mother to tell her what he saw. When we got back to the house, her mother slapped Helen and there was a massive argument. There was a lot of screaming and shouting and I felt uneasy and very vulnerable waiting at the top of the steps outside her front door. I didn't want to make the situation worse by getting involved so I kept out of it. In the end, Maria kicked us both out. I wasn't bothered as we stayed together in a hotel in Piraeus and it was a chance to be on my own with Helen without being disturbed. Maria had phoned Helen the following morning, apologising and telling her to come home.

I had to smile. "I'll never forget when we went back the next day," I told Helen. "I had the biggest smile on my face!"

Helen smiled too. "And look at us now," she said. "We have a baby. Maybe that's why my mother shouted at me. We did much more than kissing and holding hands!" Reminiscing had helped to calm Helen down after the unpleasant phone call. I reassured her that her mother couldn't harm us here in England and anyway, we were married and we had our own life. A few days later, her mother rang again and this time it was a pleasant phone call which surprised me. Helen told me later her mother had been upset about her leaving Greece the way she did. I found that very strange as Maria had tried everything to destroy our relationship while I was in Athens. I chastised myself. If Maria was trying to build bridges and mend fences, I ought to be more charitable.

Helen said her mum's attitude had changed when she knew she had a grandchild. "Guess what. She wants us all to visit her as a family."

"What a load of bollocks!" I said and Helen understood exactly what I meant as her English was excellent by then.

The phone calls carried on most nights and Helen started to get close to her mother again. I just let them get on with it. As long as Helen was happy, I didn't mind, but I didn't trust her mother one little bit. We just carried on with our life and I certainly didn't have any intentions of going to Greece again. I didn't fancy waking up in a hospital bed or being found dead on some spare ground in Athens. Christopher used to sleep next to our bed in his little crib I didn't mind feeding him while Helen had some rest. I used to look at him all the time. I just couldn't believe I was a father.

As the days went by he started to smile. Helen used to say he's had wind but I was adamant he smiled at me.

The greatest thing in my life after marrying Helen was my son Christopher saying, "Dada." I was so proud and so happy. If there was a wish I could have made, it was to be married to a beautiful girl and to have a beautiful baby boy. All my wishes and prayers had been answered. My life had changed for the better. All the wrongs that had happened to me and all the wrongs I did myself had been forgotten. I was happy and contented in my life. Little did I know that my dreams would be shattered and my nightmares would return, with a vengeance.

Chapter twenty three

The perfect family?

Over the next four years there were two major events in our lives. Christopher was growing into the most delightful little boy and giving great pleasure to Helen and me and to my mother and Jack and all the family.

The other event, which crept up on me without me really realising was the increasing closeness between Helen and her mother Maria.

All this is related in great detail in my first book, *For the Love of Christopher*. This culminated in Helen suddenly and shockingly asking me for a divorce. However, this incomprehensible request was withdrawn and I thought we had regained our earlier happiness.

Then I was persuaded by Helen that the three of us should have a family visit to her mother Maria and her husband Vangelis in Athens. Although I was far from happy about this suggestion, I thought it would make Helen happier again so I agreed.

The entire story of what transpired is related in detail in *For the Love of Christopher*. Suffice it to say that Maria had persuaded Helen to take Christopher away from me and to stay with our son in Greece. So once they were out of my reach and out of Maria's house, I was ordered to leave at once and told I would never see my wife or child again.

Despite help and advice from the British Embassy and a sympathetic Greek policeman, I was forced to return back home to England alone and heartbroken.

There then followed years of legal struggles to recover at least some of my paternal rights which after many setbacks resulted in me gaining the right to see my son but only in Greece.

After my own difficult childhood days and many setbacks, I thought I had found true happiness in the perfect family unit of my wife Helen and son Christopher. To have all this snatched away from me so brutally made me nearly end my own life but instead I resolved to fight for the son I loved, no matter how long the battle would be.

However, I never thought that I could ever again have a normal happy life.

Why did you go away?
When we first met, we fell in love
On an island in the sun
And on a hot summers day
We danced the night away
We kissed and watched the waves crashing against the rocks.
We watched the birds fly in the summer sky
Our love was new and our hearts were high
The days were young
And the nights were long
When we kissed the days stood still

We walked hand in hand in the heat of the day
And I told you I loved you so.
Then the day came and you went away
My heart was broken and my tears would flow

If you had stayed
I could have made the days like no others
We could have talked to the trees
Listened to the night birds sing

We could have sailed the seas and ridden the waves
Flown with the wind
But you went away
I flew home all alone
All I have are the memories
Empty spaces and all I see is your face

Why did you go away?
When I loved you so
I have nothing left
Just an empty room
You took the sun away
All I have is darkness

Why did you go away?
I miss the smile on your face

Chapter twenty four

Suzi

After a failed suicide attempt and the struggles I had endured in the Greek courts, I was worrying that I would never see my son Christopher again. I decided I needed time out from all the aggravation and upset. I wanted to be normal like everybody else, without all the pressures and worries. I was mentally exhausted and I thought to myself I needed a good time and a laugh.

It was Saturday and I knew Bolton would be buzzing on a Saturday night with all the pubs packed to the rafters with both sexes. It was a chance to have a dance in the nightclubs until the early hours. It was an opportunity I didn't want to miss. I rang my mate Julian and asked him if he fancied a night out in Bolton? To my relief he said yes.

We met up in Yates Wine Bar which was on Bradshawgate. It was only seven pm and the night was young. We were both knocking back the drinks and dancing on the small dance floor and just generally having a good time. I saw plenty of old friends who were pleased to see me and we chatted about old times. I deliberately didn't mention Greece. I was trying to put it to the back of mind. I was having fun. The evening was passing quickly; it was now 11pm and I didn't want the night to end. For the first time in ages I was enjoying myself so I said to Julian, why don't we both go the Icon? This was a nightclub and was open until the early hours.

We made our way to the Icon and when we arrived there were hundreds of people outside queuing up. Julian turned around, grumbled and said, "Come on Ian, let's go somewhere else. There's too many queuing up and it will be ages before we get in."

I just told him be patient; we were there. I'm glad I did because that night I met the girl who would mend my broken heart and give me love and the family I had always yearned for.

We both eventually got in and we headed straight for the bar. It was there that I met a girl by accident by knocking her drink on to the floor. I picked the glass up and was very apologetic. I just looked at her, she was absolutely stunning. She had long brown hair and a face that wouldn't look out of place on the catwalk. She was wearing a short black dress with black high-heeled shoes and a figure to die for.

She spoke to me in her soft southern accent and said, "My name is Suzi."

I replied, "My name is Ian." Suzi was with her sister Helen and her workmate Sam. She told me it was her birthday and said, "Why don't you join us?"

I could see Julian watering at the mouth so I just replied, "It will be a pleasure."

Suzi told me she was twenty-two and I bit my lip and told her I was thirty-nine fully expecting her to walk away. I was sure she would think that there was too much of an age difference. But to my surprise and relief she just smiled. We hit if off straight away and we danced till the early hours. Julian didn't do too well but it wasn't for the want of trying. However, neither Suzi's sister, Helen, nor her workmate Sam fancied him.

At the end of the night Suzi gave me her phone number and told me it was up to me if I wanted to see her again.

I walked her to her taxi and we just kissed and had a small cuddle and said our goodbyes.

I enjoyed the evening and as I was walking home my thoughts kept going back to Suzi. I was thinking to myself how pretty she was, how warm she was and what fun she was to be with. I felt totally relaxed about the situation even though I was still married to Helen.

I never expected to hear from Suzi again but to my surprise I received a phone call of her and she asked me if I wanted to see her again?

I just replied, "Yes of course," and we started to see each other on a regular basis. I felt now was the time to tell Suzi I was married and had a child. I invited her to my house in Alder Street, Great Lever.

As the night approached when she was coming, I was very worried what to say to her. I thought if I told I was married and had a child I wouldn't see her again. My house was full of memories with pictures of Helen and Christopher all over the walls. I decided to leave them on as she would notice them straight away and it would make it easier for me to tell her.

Suzi arrived on time and I was very nervous as I didn't know what kind of reaction I would get from her. I had made a special meal consisting of lamb and mashed potatoes with all the usual vegetables. The desert was a homemade apple pie and I had bought a bottle of the best vintage wine to top it off.

I heard a knock on the door and my legs went like jelly. I opened the door and there was Suzi. She gave me a little kiss and then handed me a bottle of red wine.

I put some music on hoping it would make the night more relaxing. I could see Suzi looking at the pictures on the wall so I just came straight out with it. I told her I was married with a child but my wife had left me and abducted my child in Greece. I started to break down. It was then that

Suzi took me in her arms. I just looked at her. My eyes were all puffed-up and tears where flowing down the side of my face. I told her that my marriage was over and I was just fighting in the courts to bring my son home. I was going to say to her that I would understand if she walked away but she put her finger on my mouth to stop me speaking. It was then that we just started kissing and before we knew it we were in bed making love. She stayed all night and I felt totally relaxed about the situation.

We got on so well together. She was a breath of fresh air and a shoulder to cry on. She was the one who had picked me up when I was down. She stood by me when it was easier to walk away from my troubles and depressions. Our relationship grew from strength to strength under very difficult circumstances.

I really cared for Suzi and the first big test of our relationship was when I went to Greece in February 1999. I went with the some reporters from the Bolton Evening News and we were all arrested after visiting Helen's house. It was all over the TV and the local paper and all the billboards around Bolton. I wasn't locked up, unlike the two reporters, so I was able to telephone Suzi and tell her not to worry as I was fine. She was crying and it was then that she told me for the very first time that she loved me and that she was worried about me. I told her I loved her too and that I would soon be home.

Suzi and I would become inseparable. She would stand shoulder to shoulder with me in the Greek courts. In the end we won a great victory for access to see my son Christopher in Greece. It was in the Greek courts that Suzi met Helen for the very first time and it was also there that she handed Helen the divorce papers which, up till then, she had refused to sign.

In October 2000 we decided to get married. The time was right as by then I was divorced from Helen and the court battles had ended. I was able to see Christopher in Greece and be a father to him after my access victory in court. Suzi not only stood by me she fought my corner in the Greek courts for which I will always be truly grateful. She accompanied me to Greece and built a special relationship with my son Christopher not just in Greece but in England as well.

We now have two beautiful children of our own, Amy Louise who was born in 2002 and Adam my younger son born in 2005.

We are now a real family. That is what I had always longed for. At the time of writing this story, we have been together for nearly 15 years.

I can now look back on many fond memories of Suzi. She is by my side and has confronted my demons of the past. I can never thank her enough for standing by me through all the difficult times.

There are just three words that say how much she means to me, "Suzi, I love you xx,"

Happy at Last

Epilogue

I was at work and it was during a short break that I was discussing my first book with a work colleague.

He asked me why I had missed so much out of *For the Love of Christopher* about my own early life. From that moment I was determined to write a book about those early days.

My first bad memory was feeling the wrath of my father. I was four years old at the time. I was sitting in the kitchen talking to my mother, when the door opened; it was my father. I held out my hands and called. "Dad," and smiled. His response was to walk over to punch me in the face, knocking me over the Table. I would never forget the look of horror on my mother's face. Over the next few years throughout my childhood; crying on my school desk, looking at the clock every Friday night, frightened not of the bogey man but of someone who was real, my father.

The beatings carried on until I was sixteen but it all came to a sudden end when I finally stood up to him.

I blame my father for the troubles in my life which sent me on a path of self-destruction, of petty crime and football violence, when all I wanted was to be loved by my family.

If this abuse had happened today, the social services would have intervened and my father would have been dealt with. Instead, I rebelled against my father and the system and I ran away to Paris because I was I afraid.

I Joined the French Foreign Legion living a dream which quickly turned into a nightmare. Then I joined the British Army only to rebel against the hierarchy. Suffering from failed relationships and then the death of my father, made me realise that my life needed to change.

So I went on a journey and fell in love with a Greek girl called Helen in Corfu, Greece. I would finally marry her and have a son called Christopher who later would be abducted by Helen and her family on a planned holiday at her family home in Athens, Greece in 1998.

After a failed suicide attempt I decided to carry on the fight in the Greek courts and I would finally win access to my son. He finally came to England in 2011 for the first time since 1998.

When I finally got divorced from Helen I married a Kent girl called Suzi, in October 2000.

She stood by me through the all the battles in the Greek courts and give me the confidence to love again. We now have two children Amy Louise and Adam. I finally have the family unit I always craved for.

The author with Amy Louise & Adam